# BATTERED

# BATTERED

## The Abuse of Children

MARGARET JAY *and* SALLY DOGANIS

Weidenfeld and Nicolson

LONDON

Copyright © by Margaret Jay and Sally Doganis 1987

All rights reserved. No part of this publication
may be reproduced, stored in a retrieval system, or
transmitted, in any form or by any means, electronic,
mechanical, photocopying, recording or otherwise,
without the prior permission of the copyright holder.

First published in Great Britain by
George Weidenfeld & Nicolson Limited
91 Clapham High Street
London SW4 7TA

Printed and bound in Great Britain by
Butler & Tanner Ltd, Frome and London

ISBN 0 297 79215 6 cased
ISBN 0 297 79256 3 paper

# CONTENTS

Introduction                                    vii

1   A Charter for Children                        1

2   Family Ties                                  22

3   The Lethal Family                            44

4   Neglect                                      61

5   Witness for the Prosecution                  80

6   Listening to the Children                   100

7   The Psychological Time Bomb                 126

8   The Survivors and the Cycle                 150

9   The Dutch Solution                          173

10  'It Shouldn't Hurt to Be a Child'           197

# INTRODUCTION

As journalists we first became concerned about child abuse when we reported on the public inquiry into the death of four-year-old Jasmine Beckford, who had been battered to death by her stepfather. The investigation into her life and death, which followed the highly publicized trial of her parents, focused general attention on child abuse. Suddenly there was a flood of media stories about a toddler starved to death in an empty room, about a baby whose body was covered with human bites or a little girl who was kidnapped and repeatedly raped; and, most recently, a four-year-old who was kicked to death in what has been described as a 'uniquely wicked crime'.

We continued our interest with a television documentary on the increasing problem of child sexual abuse. We showed that more and more sexual abuse was being uncovered and argued that British legal practice made the child a victim not only of the traumatic abuse but of the legal system itself. We compared the British system to that of the USA, which is more sympathetic to children's rights, and illustrated in some detail the system in Texas, which allows children to relate their experiences on video, rather than appear in court. We realized then that much of the material concerning the handling of child abuse in Britain and abroad was uncharted and unknown, and so we decided to get behind the headlines – headlines which have grown increasingly dramatic as the balance between parental rights and protecting children from abuse has become violently controversial.

What is the truth? Is child abuse really a new social problem that has exploded in the 1980s? How are the doctors, social workers and other professional experts trying to cope with it?

What powers do they have in order to try to protect children who may be at risk? And what of the perpetrators and the victims of abuse? Why do adults assault children and how do the children who survive physically deal with the trauma of abuse?

This book is our report on these inquiries. It is a book written by journalists for the general reader but, in our researches, we drew heavily on the expert guidance of many people whose professional lives are spent in this field. We would like particularly to thank Dr Arnon Bentovim of Great Ormond Street Hospital, London; Dr Eileen Vizard of Newham Child Guidance, London; Dr Jane Wynne, Consultant Paediatrician of Leeds Royal Infirmary; Dr Leonard Taitz, Consultant Paediatrician at Sheffield Children's Hospital; Rose Rackman of the London School of Economics; Ken Boyce, Director of Social Services for the London Borough of Newham; Steve Roe, Chris Chaston and Jed McAndrew in the Nottingham social services department (and we would like to thank those other social services departments who wish to remain anonymous, for their readiness to open their files); Dr Chris Hobbs of St James University Hospital, Leeds; Dr Arend Jan Koers and Dr Cees De Waal of the Confidential Doctor programme in Holland; Susan Creighton, Research Officer of the NSPCC; David Larter of the London Borough of Redbridge social services department; Professor Cyril Greenland; Steve Chaney, Prosecuting Attorney, Fort Worth, Texas; and Gail Goodman, Professor of Psychology, University of Denver, Colorado.

Catherine Boyd, Ben Neild and Pat Campbell also contributed to the original ideas and research.

We have dealt at length with many different cases of child abuse; some of them – Malcolm Page, Maria Colwell, Denis O'Neill and Jasmine Beckford – have already been the subject of published reports and inquiries, but in every other case information was given to us on a confidential basis and in these cases, although the details are factual, the names of parents, children and social workers have been changed and places have been disguised. We would like to thank the people involved for the frankness with which they were prepared to talk about their experiences.

Margaret Jay and Sally Doganis

*May 1987*

# 1 A CHARTER FOR CHILDREN

Every time we – parents, press, general public – learn about a sickening case of child abuse we react with shocked surprise. Each case seems to strike like a bombshell, an apparently unexpected disaster to be treated as an individual tragedy. There is something deep in all of us which is unwilling to accept that the battered child is, and probably always has been, a constant, albeit hidden, part of family life. Year by year, in our increasingly open society, the statisticians produce figures which show that there is more abuse – more physical violence, more neglect, more sexual exploitation – and then the experts argue about whether the problem has really got worse or is just better reported. Politicians and moralists debate whether this is another deplorable result of social stress, bad education and unemployment, or a sign of declining standards in personal behaviour and the collapse of the traditional family. But public attention is shortlived. After the initial outrage which greets yet another notorious disaster when a child dies or the publication of yet another set of alarming figures, we all seem to sink back into unaccepting apathy, only to be temporarily aroused again by the next horrifying episode.

Our refusal to look at child abuse as a continuing, ever present phenomenon, the way we hope we are witnessing a chapter of accidents, stems partly from a deep-seated revulsion. We shrink from hearing details about fractured small bones, little bodies that are hungry and dirty, or innocent sex organs that have been violated, and find it less painful just to turn away and try to avoid hearing about another case. Discussion of child abuse is

still taboo, and public debate is often couched in circumspect
and inexact terms which are out of place in a world where other
intimate experiences of family life are handled with almost
abrasive candour. But our taboos are based as much on strong
historical traditions about children as they are on today's aesthetic sensitivities about cruelty and degradation. For many
centuries children were regarded as part of their parents' property, and therefore it was totally acceptable that parents should
treat their offspring exactly as they wanted to. As Henry and
Ruth Kempe, the American children's doctors who first identified child abuse, have written, 'If an investigator were trans-
ported back to the nineteenth century so that he could survey
the family scene with modern eyes, child abuse would be clearly
visible to him. In the past, however, it was largely invisible to
families and their communities.... Historically society has not
been troubled by the maltreatment of children.'

Even from a contemporary perspective, many of us are probably insensitive to historical abuse. It is comfortable to believe
that the harsh taskmasters who sent children up chimneys and
down mines, and the mothers who regularly committed infan-
ticide to limit the size of their families, were part of an unen-
lightened strand of social history and not deliberately abusive
adults of the kind we are forced to recognize today. We know
that generations of children were openly battered by their
parents in the interests of discipline; literally 'beating the devil
out' was a common practice condoned by society. Today, the
majority would reject such violent corporal punishment, but
there are still disputes about the degree of physical chastisement
a parent may legitimately inflict on a child, and about whether
anyone except a parent should make that judgement about any
child. Changing attitudes to child abuse have been affected by
both cultural and economic advances which have stopped the exploitation of very young labour, reduced the more grotesque
elements of homelessness and destitution, and generally
increased the value of human life. In addition, there is widespread agreement that children may have individual rights. Even
to admit that possibility, however, challenges fundamental
assumptions about the inviolate authority of parents over their
children which has formed the basis of family organization in
the past. It is not surprising that we are uneasy about tackling

a subject which directly raises these basic questions, and that the taboos which presume that life within a family is private and protected are still alive. They make it possible for us to continue to ignore everything except the most flagrant abuse which, when it is revealed, we can treat as an aberration.

But if Dr Henry Kempe's 'modern investigator' reported to us on some of the less obvious aspects of nineteenth-century child abuse, which could be identified with the benefit of recent knowledge, we would see clear patterns which have continued in a straight line for a hundred years. As early as 1868, a London paediatric surgeon wrote about the high number of recurring fractures in his young patients' limbs. He attributed these to rickets, the nutritional deficiency disease which causes bones to become very fragile, and which was prevalent among the poor sections of the population. Few questions were asked about the fractures. It was assumed that an inadequate diet made the bones so delicate that they snapped easily and often. Today's experts are far less sanguine about this simple physical explanation, and assert that most of the children who suffered repeated fractures in the 1860s were being battered. However, it is only in the last twenty-five years that experts have been prepared confidently to make this diagnosis. The rickets myth long outlived the improvements in living standards which made it an unlikely explanation for broken bones.

It was after the Second World War that improvements in the quality of x-rays enabled radiologists to begin to distinguish between arms and legs that had been deliberately broken and those which had been injured in other ways. One American radiologist noticed that the children with suspected traumatic bone fractures often had another symptom, a type of brain swelling, which he thought could be caused by shaking. It was additional evidence that the child might have been injured by his parents or by someone else looking after him; the previously unthinkable possibility that children regularly suffered physical assult in their own homes began to be discussed by academic paediatricians.

In 1961 Henry Kempe, a children's doctor in Denver, Colorado, organized a presentation at the annual conference of American Paediatricians on what he called, for the first time, 'The Battered Child Syndrome'. Kempe described this as 'a term used by us to characterize a clinical condition in young children who have received physical abuse generally from a parent or a guardian'. The presentation included reports from hospitals all over America of children being treated for the type of conditions that the radiologists now regarded as suspicious. The following year the *Journal of the American Medical Association* published the findings of Kempe's presentation and additional material which looked at some of the psychological and legal implications of the medical problem doctors saw themselves confronted with. The article recommended that doctors should report all cases to the police so that punitive action could be taken against the perpetrators. Through one seminal piece Dr Kempe and his colleagues had succeeded in identifying the battered child both as a medical phenomenon, who should have special treatment, and as the victim of a crime. Knowledge spread slowly, however, and Dr Kempe's ideas were resisted by many doctors who still found it extremely difficult to accept that parental violence was as widespread and as damaging as was suggested.

In Britain expert radiologists picked up their American colleagues' research and began to look for similar types of injury. In 1963 Dr D. I. Griffiths and Dr. F. J. Moynihan collaborated to publish a learned article entitled 'Multiple Epiphyseal Injuries in Babies: The Battered Baby Syndrome', and so another chilling expression had been coined. British radiologists and paediatricians were given support by forensic pathologists, who had the grim task of examining the bodies of babies and children who had died in what were considered possibly unnatural circumstances. They were detached from the professional concerns which made many doctors unwilling to breach their patients' confidentiality and become involved with legal proceedings. They were perfectly prepared to make categorical judgements that children had been violently killed and had not died in a tragic accident as parents so often insisted.

Anyone who has read a post-mortem report on a battered child will not be surprised to learn that pathologists were so indignant about what they saw that they became pioneering leaders of the campaign to get physical abuse recognized for what it was. The forensic pathologist who conducted the 1984 post-mortem of four-year-old Jasmine Beckford, the most publicized victim of recent years, listed four pages of injuries that the little girl had suffered at the hands of her stepfather, including recently fractured ribs, fractures of the pelvis and of the pubic bones on both sides, and multiple scars of old fractures all over her body. The pathologist noted: 'the x-ray appearances of the bones did not suggest that they were unusually brittle'.

The pathologist's report concluded:

> Jasmine Beckford was a very thin little girl who had died as a result of severe head injuries. Natural disease appears to have played no part in her death.
>
> There were multiple old scars on the deceased's body consistent with repeated episodes of physical abuse. There were numerous fresh injuries on the deceased's body consistent with the effects of a severe physical beating conducted within the period of a day or so leading up to her death. There were marks which included injuries such as might be left by slaps and punches and some of the injuries to the face were consistent with the effects of hard punches.
>
> The fatal brain injury had been caused by blows to the child's head.

The lay person's common-sense reaction to such a report is that the child had obviously been the victim of deliberate assault. Yet in the days before medical science had acquired more sophisticated methods of analysis, and before Dr Kempe and his followers had changed the cultural climate so that the possibility of deliberate violence was at last considered, a different explanation of death might have been accepted, even in a case as extreme as that of Jasmine Beckford.

It is significant, given the emphasis today on child abuse as a social problem, that all the impetus for change in the 1960s came from medical sources. The doctors exposed their own old myths about rickets and accidental deaths, and adopted the word 'syndrome', suggesting an illness, to describe a battered child. The medical profession tried, through their articles and lectures, to spread understanding to the wider community, but the underlying assumption was that this was a problem for medicine. Today there are still many doctors who believe that they should be given the primary role in deciding whether a child has been abused and how the child should be treated. Dr Leonard Taitz, a Sheffield paediatrician, stated in his evidence to the Inquiry into the death of Jasmine Beckford in 1985, 'The criteria for removing children from their parents, the criteria for returning them, the criteria for monitoring them wherever they are living are essentially medical.' But in the twenty-five years since the battered-child syndrome was discovered the problem of abuse has become much greater than broken bones, and the problems of diagnosis and management have become more complex as a result.

Over the last quarter of a century the 'battered child' has gradually been relabelled the 'abused child' as society has realized that children can be sexually mistreated and consistently neglected in a way that is as damaging to normal development as physical assault.

There has always been concern about neglect; even in the days when abusive fractures were diagnosed as rickets the community was aware that some children were deprived of food, shelter and affection at home. Society has tried to protect children from parents who are either unable or unwilling to look after their offspring adequately, but has often found it difficult to define the boundaries of neglect. Precisely because neglect is a refusal to act (the absence of proper care) rather than an act of aggression, outsiders have been extremely chary of intervening in families which, they feel, may just have different habits and attitudes from their own.

It was only in 1980 that the Department of Health and Social Security (DHSS) felt sufficiently confident about the analyses of emotional deprivation and neglect to bring them into formal child-abuse procedures. Key guidelines were then issued which stipulated that children who were neglected were 'at risk' and must be registered as in need of special attention, as battered children had been for many years. Very recently the National Society for the Prevention of Cruelty to Children (NSPCC) has launched a major campaign to focus attention on the suffering caused by neglect, and to urge people to abandon their inhibitions about interfering in the way 'other people handle their children' and to be more vigilant and energetic about distinguishing those parents who are cheerfully casual, ill-kempt or disorganized from those who are abusive.

Sexual abuse has only just begun to be acknowledged in the

1980s; it has been the most closely guarded family secret of them all. Experts in the subject have suggested to us that today's understanding of sexual abuse is at about the same stage as the understanding of physical abuse was just after Dr Henry Kempe published his work in 1962. In other words, we are only starting to uncover and come to terms with the problem. Following the previous pattern we are at the moment seeing an enormous upsurge in the numbers of cases reported, accompanied by agitated public concern at what is feared to be another sign of the extreme depravity of the modern world. Very recently there has been equal concern that over-zealous investigation may be 'discovering' abuse where none exists, but the weight of expert opinion is adamant that as many as one in ten children may suffer some form of sexual abuse. Dr Jane Wynne, a Leeds paediatrician who has become a leading national consultant in this field, has, typically, seen her personal case-book grow from no sexually abused children at all at the end of the 1970s to nearly 200 seven years later, but she rejects the idea that there are actually more children being sexually abused than previously. 'I think it's just that we are recognizing it more,' she told us. 'We're all getting much better at picking up the signs – not just doctors, but nursery nurses, teachers, social workers. We're all listening to children and hearing what they are saying. We didn't listen before because we just couldn't bear to. That's part of the problem. It's very, very difficult to acknowledge that an adult would use a child for his own gratification, which is what sexual abuse is all about.'

In one generation professional understanding about the nature and scope of child abuse has been transformed, and public awareness of the problem, which had been hidden behind the walls of family privacy, has gradually developed. The steady growth in expert knowledge, accompanied by sporadic general interest, usually responding to reports of particularly horrible cases, has happened during a period when attitudes to the family, to personal morality and to social welfare have been very volatile. In the 1960s, when the battered child was 'discovered', Britain was in an optimistic mood, and the cultural liberation of that time, which went with a sense of economic security, caused a relaxation in family structures and a lowering of the barricades surrounding the Englishman's castle. At one and the same time this allowed for much greater openness in confronting issues such as child abuse, and added to the social stresses which sometimes lead to that abuse. Since the 1960s there have been more broken marriages, more single-parent families and more common-law relationships, where young children may find themselves living with several successive father-figures. All of these changes have imposed extra strains on the complicated job of child-rearing.

At the beginning of this period most of us were pretty confident that the agencies of our well-organized welfare state would cope with the casualties and deal successfully with the newly emerging phenomenon of the battered child. The 1970s and 1980s, however, have clouded both the personal and the social optimism; we have seen economic hardship and unemployment compounding the difficulties of many families. Simultaneously, public resources for the agencies who might have helped these families have been cut and the competence of those agencies has been regularly challenged. Some political voices have called for more self-help and a return to Victorian family values, a complete swing of the pendulum from the free-flowing assumptions of twenty years ago. Rapidly changing opinions have been reflected in new and different family law and the changing organization of welfare services for children. And, as every type of child abuse has apparently become more prevalent, there has been a growing feeling that there are things fundamentally wrong with current theory and practice. Critics have focused particularly on the local authority social services departments, who often assume responsibility for children considered to be vulnerable at home.

Social services departments as we know them today have been in existence only since 1971, and their development has coincided with the growing understanding of child abuse. Today, because we regard the general problem as a social one and not as the strictly medical syndrome of the original diagnosis, inadequate social work is often blamed when another bad case of abuse come to light. The instinctive response of the public and the media is to make social workers the scapegoats, particularly when a child who is already known to be in danger dies or is badly injured. An official study of social workers published in 1982 concluded, 'Too much is generally expected of social workers. We load upon them unrealistic expectations and then complain when they don't live up to them.' Our conversations with practising social workers and their managers suggest that they vehemently support this assessment, particularly in the intractable, stressful field of child abuse. It can be argued that, at precisely the time when the battered child was recognized as an acute problem by the world outside the academic communities, the social services were reorganized in a way that reduced the specialist skills needed to cope with the numbers of new cases. Equally, when one considers the notorious series of scandals that have been analysed and inquired into over the last twenty years it is hard to escape the conclusion that many of the same mistakes have been made repeatedly and the lessons of those mistakes have been almost carelessly unheeded.

It was a scandal of a very familiar kind which created an impetus for the first piece of post-war legislation designed to protect children from ill-treatment. In 1945 twelve-year-old Denis O'Neill died after being badly beaten at a farm in Shropshire where he was being 'boarded out' by Newport Council, South Wales, which had him in their care. A post-mortem revealed that the boy had been undernourished and generally a victim of physical neglect, and Denis's foster-parents were subsequently convicted of manslaughter and child neglect.

Denis and his younger brother had been sent away from their home town of Newport to the rural village of Minsterly in Shropshire, thus moving from the jurisdiction of one council to that of another. Each authority assumed that the other was responsible for overseeing the brothers. No one checked up on them properly and the farmer foster-parents clearly regarded the boys as slave labourers. The case attracted considerable publicity and the Home Secretary of the time set up an inquiry which was conducted by a distinguished lawyer and politician, Sir Walter Monckton, who sat alone and heard evidence for only four days, in contrast with some of the lengthy tribunals which have recently been held. His report was very critical of both the local authorities concerned, and he recommended that 'the personal relation in which the public authority, which has undertaken care and protection, stands to the children should be more clearly recognized'. Significantly, forty years later another distinguished lawyer, Louis Blom-Cooper, in his report on the death of Jasmine Beckford, approvingly quoted this point from Sir Walter Monckton, and added 'these words could be ours'.

In 1945 no one spoke of 'a battered child' or the 'syndrome of abuse' – this was seventeen years before Dr Henry Kempe first published his ideas – but Monckton's report, which created agitation in Parliament, led to the Curtis Committee on the Care of Children and then to the Children Act in 1948. It was the beginning of a parallel development: on the one hand, a development of interest in how the new post-war welfare state could best intervene to look after children whom the community judged to be badly treated, and on the other hand a development of the medical interest in looking at domestic injuries with a more sceptical eye.

The 1948 Children Act, passed by the reforming Labour government elected three years before, was in line with the other new social welfare laws in attempting to centralize and control services and organizations which had previously been randomly divided between statutory, private and voluntary arrangements. The Act instructed each local authority to set up a Children's Committee, and to appoint a Children's Officer, who had to be approved by the Secretary of State. This senior official was responsible for organizing and maintaining all the services for the care and protection of children in his jurisdiction and, according to the Act, 'shall not, except with the authority of the Secretary of State, be employed in any other capacity'. Local authorities were obliged to recruit teams of specialized staff to assist the senior officer, who were also exclusively employed to deal with matters relating to children. The government hoped that by setting up a powerful system of this kind they could avoid the problems highlighted in the Monckton report by making the lines of responsibility for a child like Denis O'Neill very clear and by constantly emphasizing that the new organization was designed to help children, thus underlining the need for officials to relate primarily to those children.

The question of residential care and fostering was one of the basic issues which was looked at in a different way as a result of the new emphasis on children's needs. Residential nurseries and homes for older children, organized by both local authorities and charities such as Dr Barnardo's, continued, but modern ideas about child-rearing and psychology lent support to the increasingly popular view that, if possible, a substitute home must always be preferred to long-term care in an institution.

The Children's Officers kept on the children's homes as a useful resource, particularly for children needing a short-term base while crises were dealt with or their situations assessed. In some cases, particularly where a series of fostering arrangements had broken down and a child could be accommodated in a small, intimate local authority home, the Children's Officers preferred the long-term stability of such an arrangement to another set of potentially impermanent substitute parents.

Over the years, however, the residential institution has become anathema to most professional social workers, and such homes have just been allowed to fade away. Today few authorities maintain more than a handful of places and the only options for children at risk in their own homes are either for them to be fostered, not always an easy solution, or for them to be kept with their own parents under close supervision. In their report on the death of Jasmine Beckford the panel of inquiry said that the social workers had 'an innate hostility' to residential care and did not even consider it as a possible alternative for Jasmine and her little sister, who were both thought to be at risk at home. The Children's Officers of the 1948 Act would have found this attitude very surprising. They regarded residential homes as just another weapon in their formidable armoury to deal with children in their care.

In retrospect the provisions of the 1948 Act have been criticized as too authoritarian and heavy-handed, but its supporters point out that during the twenty-two years of its operation there were no major scandals regarding maltreated children in local authority care. Many of those who worked in the system still feel that their power to take decisions and the special knowledge they gained from dealing intensively with children's problems gave them enough professional confidence to make the right decisions about their clients' best interests. But child psychiatrists who have studied long-stay children's homes, and adults who now look back on many years spent in them, are unhappy about the lack of individual care and nurturing they provided and fear that there are permanent emotional scars; on the other hand, the residents were never physically neglected or battered to death, as they might have been in their own homes.

No doubt the Children's Officer sometimes made sweeping judgements, but at least anyone who reviewed those judgements could be sure that they were the opinions of a child-care specialist who was specifically enjoined to give the child the highest priority. The 1948 Act created a strong, relatively simple structure which was well suited to the directional organization of the early welfare state, but it did not survive the different attitudes towards social work that grew up in the 1960s, and the subsequent demise of Children's Officers has often been regretted by those concerned with child abuse.

In 1968 the Committee on Local Authority and Allied Personal Social Services, chaired by the banker Frederic Seebohm, produced a report which was accepted and acted on by Harold Wilson's Labour government. It radically altered the whole structure of social services in every area. 'The first necessity', the report stated, 'is to introduce a unified social services department within each local authority.' The aim was to bring under one management the different agencies which looked after the old, the mentally and physically handicapped, those with housing or benefit problems, and, of course, the children. 'This will provide a community-based and family-oriented service, which will be available to all. This department will reach beyond the discovery and rescue of social casualties; it will enable the greatest number of individuals to act reciprocally, giving and receiving service for the well-being of the whole community.'

The Seebohm philosophy stemmed from a wish to deal with family problems in a comprehensive way, to look at the family as a unit, not to deal with different members individually. Hitherto both welfare officers and their clients had complained that they were giving a fragmented service, with perhaps several agencies visiting one household; now there would be one social worker who, theoretically at least, would be able to handle all the difficulties. The wish to deal with the family in a unified way went hand in hand with a strong feeling that more efficient, and less costly, social services could be offered by reducing expensive institutional care and creating a more extensive network of community support. Families should be kept together and given adequate help to look after each other at home. Acute crises could therefore be prevented.

Seebohm recommended that there should be a greater number of professional social workers, and that they should be assisted by improved local services, such as home helps, meals on wheels, play facilities and babysitters. The report recognized that all this would need considerable resources, but argued that in the long run it would prevent social problems and be cost-effective because the decreasing number of casualties would free resources for more preventive measures. One chapter of the report concluded: 'We are convinced that an effective health service, sufficient decent housing, full employment, adequate incomes and an imaginative and well-developed education system are the cornerstones of any general preventative policy to avoid social distress.' From the perspective of the 1980s this sounds naively optimistic but the theory was in tune with contemporary assumptions about the constantly improving quality of life, and legislation to set up the new system was rapidly passed.

With hindsight we believe that the conspicuous failures to understand and manage the complex problems of child abuse, which in recent years have brought calumny upon many social services departments and destroyed the reputations of well-meaning social workers, stem directly from the organizational changes created after the Seebohm report and from the attitudes to family policy which those changes reflected. The new social services departments were deliberately made up of non-specialist 'generic' social workers, who were trained to handle a wide range of cases and not to become narrowly committed to any one aspect of their profession. This has meant, in practice, that the kinds of specialist skills needed to deal with child abuse have never been taught to students and that each qualified social worker has such a wide range of responsibilities that he or she never gains the concentrated experience which would more than compensate for inadequate theoretical knowledge. The old-fashioned expertise of the Children's Officer has gone.

At the same time the social theory of dealing with the whole family collectively has often resulted in children being given a lower priority than they received when they were handled by their own particular welfare agency. A busy social worker beset by a number of problems afflicting a client family may well find it easier to deal with the problems presented by the adults and to judge apparent changes in the family situation by contact with those with whom it is most easy to communicate. The vital need for a personal relationship between a social worker and a child who may be at risk of abuse was emphasized in the Denis O'Neill report in 1945, and stressed yet again by the Jasmine Beckford report in 1985, but it seems often to be ignored by the generic social worker. Time after time we have read reports where a social worker failed to talk to or make any direct contact with a child, failed even to observe the child closely, and therefore missed the signs of abuse which a specialist devoted exclusively to the interests of the child would have noticed.

Ironically, the Seebohm Committee themselves put forward the best argument against the changes which they themselves recommended. The case for maintaining the existing system, they said, was based on the claim that 'the present patterns of organization and the kinds of specialization and training which they embody have evolved in response to needs (for example Children's Officers to deal specifically with children) and that evolution on this basis should be allowed to continue and the services not forced into new moulds on the basis of theory rather than emergent and developing practice'. Unfortunately the committee did not accept this argument, and during the ensuing generation of social work based on theory the number of mis-handled child-abuse cases has multiplied.

The watershed tragedy was the death of eight-year-old Maria Colwell, beaten to death by her stepfather in 1973. The wealth of publicity which surrounded the criminal trial of her stepfather, and more especially the official inquiry that followed, focused concern on the two issues that continue to trouble the public most: the role of the social services and the rights of natural, biological parents as compared with those of foster-parents or other guardians with no blood tie to the child.

Maria Colwell was the fifth child of her mother's first marriage and her father died shortly after she was born. The Colwell family, who lived in Brighton, had a troubled history and their circumstances seemed to become much worse after Mr Colwell's death; the local authority decided to place care orders on the children in an attempt to ensure that they were properly looked after. The care orders gave total legal rights over the children to the East Sussex social services department, which had the power to decide where and with whom they should live. But Mrs Colwell made her own private arrangement to foster Maria with her late husband's sister and brother-in-law, and the social workers gave their blessing to this plan. Maria lived happily with her aunt and uncle for the next five years; here she seems to have thrived physically and to have had a perfectly normal pre-school life. She stayed in touch with her own mother, who had meanwhile married one William Keppel, and in October 1971, to the chagrin of her foster-parents, she was taken back to live with her natural family, which now included a stepfather and other children. Maria's mother then applied to have the care order revoked and, although the social workers were worried both by the disruption to Maria's settled life and by Mr Keppel's known record of violence (he was said to have 'quite a wild reputation'), they supported the legal change and simply retained supervisory powers over the little girl. The supervision order gave them much less authority to intervene and meant that, automatically, the case received reduced priority in the social workers' crowded case-books.

In the months that followed, Maria's school teachers noticed that the child was obviously unhappy and that she seemed to be the victim of an extraordinary number of 'accidents' at home. She often came to school with bruises on her arms and legs and once had a black eye which, her mother explained, had been caused by the child falling downstairs. But although these events were noted by the school there was remarkably little collaboration between the educational and social services authorities, and neither acted on this apparently clear evidence of abuse. Both were subsequently criticized for not monitoring Maria's life at home with sufficient care.

On 7 January 1973, fifteen months after she had returned to her mother's care, Maria was taken to the local hospital by Mr and Mrs Keppel in a pram; she was found to be dead on arrival. The post-mortem showed that she was severely bruised all over her body and head, and had major internal injuries in her stomach. Her injuries was said to have been caused by 'extreme violence'. Maria's body weighed only thirty-six pounds, about half the weight of a normal child of her age.

William Keppel was duly brought to trial and convicted of

murder, later reduced on appeal to manslaughter, but general interest in how and why Maria had died intensified when the Secretary of State for Social Services, Sir Keith Joseph, set up a committee of inquiry into 'The care and supervision provided by the local authorities and other agencies in relation to Maria Colwell'. Nigel Parton, a social historian, has argued persuasively that in 1973 Keith Joseph had become very interested in the issue of child abuse and had been influenced by an informal group of leading professionals in the field who called themselves the Tunbridge Wells Study Group. The Secretary of State was anxious, therefore, to put child abuse on the national agenda and deliberately organized the Colwell inquiry in a manner designed to stir up outrage and concern. The inquiry sat in public for forty-one days and heard seventy witnesses. The media devoted enormous attention to the hearings and several newspapers developed crusading campaigns about the 'Battered Baby Scandal'; it was the first time the issue had been recognized by the general public and treated as front-page material by the popular press. Keith Joseph had sensed correctly that the time was ripe for an examination of the workings of the new, post-Seebohm social services departments, which were already being criticized for inadequate efficiency in child care, only two years after being launched with great enthusiasm.

There was also growing discussion and disquiet about the overriding powers of natural parents, who seemed to be able to assert total control over a child even when his or her best interests might lie elsewhere. The significance of the natural family had been given a boost by the social policy of working with the family as a unit and handling all problems in the home, but some of these concepts were out of phase with the general trends which had grown up in the pragmatic 1960s. A society which now more readily accepted divorce and illegitimacy was less committed than previous generations to the idea that a child's only possible worthwhile home was with two biological parents and was much more willing to look at different arrangements which might provide better care.

Nevertheless, social-work practice of attempting to keep natural families together at all costs had been intellectually reinforced by the widely accepted views of distinguished child psychiatrists such as John Bowlby, who stressed the vital importance for future personality development of a child's early relationship with his mother. By the 1970s, however, the imperative need for bonding with a natural parent was being challenged by other experts who maintained that a blood tie could be adequately replaced by a psychological tie to a parent-figure not biologically related to the child but who nevertheless provided the child with stable, continuous care. The 'permanency principle', which emphasized the continuity of a relationship as the foundation for satisfactory development, gave theoretical strength to lay public opinion which was attracted to the common-sense view that a child such as Maria Colwell would have been much better left with her long-term foster-parents than returned to her natural but lethal family. The Colwell report stated categorically that 'too much emphasis has been placed on rehabilitation and preserving family ties, and parental rights have been guarded too fiercely at the expense of substitute parents and the children themselves'.

The publication of the report gave an impetus to parliamentary action in much the same way as the earlier report on Denis O'Neill had done, and in 1975 the Children Act (introduced by Dr David Owen, who was then Minister of Health in the Labour government) became law. The most important message of the new Act was that the interests of the child were not necessarily the same as those of the parents. The historically cherished belief that a child was the parents' property was formally abandoned and the notion of children's individual rights was officially sanctioned. The Act increased the powers of local authorities by making it easier for them to assume full parental rights over children thought to be at risk. Further inroads were made into the authority of natural parents by extending the grounds on which social services departments could insist that a child be adopted without parental consent; these now included cases where 'the parent has seriously ill-treated the child and the rehabilitation of the child within the household of the parents is unlikely'.

To read the terms of the 1975 Act, the debates which accompanied its passage through Parliament and the media comment of the time, leads one to assume that social workers would immediately have abandoned their practice of striving to keep hopeless families together. But, tragically, this did not happen. Ten years later Jasmine Beckford was sent back to her own parents and to her subsequent death after a happy period in foster care with a couple who were anxious to offer her a permanent home. The Blom-Cooper report judged that the 'ill-conceived programme of rehabilitation' had led inevitably to the final disaster. Now Louis Blom-Cooper is investigating the consequences of another notorious return to parental care in the case of Kimberley Carlile, who was murdered by her mother's cohabitee. Even now, long after the Beckford case, and more than a decade after Colwell, social workers still struggle on with rehabilitation, as we show later in the book, and the frustrated observer can only ask why this is so? The authors' view is that the tenacious attachment to the blood tie of natural families stems directly from the philosophy and methods of social work in the post-Seebohm unified social services departments. This attachment persists even when, as in the Colwell and Beckford cases – and with Kimberley Carlile – only one 'parent' is biologically related to the child.

A generic social worker must, by definition, look after the individual interests of each member of a client family and the collective interests of the family as a whole. It must be almost impossible, both professionally and psychologically, for any social worker to advocate the rights of one person to the detriment of others in the same family. To promote the rights of a child against the authority of the parents would, in this context, be seen as divisive and negative. Several social workers have also pointed out to us that, to be successful, their work has to be based on a trusting relationship with the people they are trying to help: their clients must see them as friendly advisers and not as threatening officials. In the experience of those professionals we have talked to, and certainly on the reported evidence of those cases which have been investigated, even the most abusive or neglectful parents are usually very resentful when they are told that their behaviour may lead to the removal of their children, and strenuously oppose any moves in that direction. Therefore, a social worker who is supposed to be working with an entire family but is seen as someone who may recommend the break-up of the family will not be trusted and will receive little co-operation.

These are genuinely difficult problems relating to the management of child abuse in the present structure of social work, and there have been other, recurring criticisms about the way in which children at risk have been handled which appear to have been caused as much by the inadequacy of those operating the system as by the shortcomings of the system itself.

Since the report on the death of Maria Colwell was published in 1974 there has been at least one major inquiry into a case of child abuse each year, and in 1982 the DHSS produced its own summary of the findings in eighteen cases which analysed all the recommendations that had been made previously. The summary showed that time and time again the reports have criticized both the lack of supervision of inexpert front-line workers involved in child abuse and the failure of social services departments to use the information which could be supplied to them by health visitors or schools or play-groups to help them make objective assessments about a child's well-being. In a system which necess-arily means that social workers who have no specific training or experience of child abuse may be asked to handle complex cases of this nature, it would seem crucial that they should receive close support and advice from their seniors. They, in turn, should be aware of valuable potential assistance from other agencies. In many of the cases analysed, however, this just did not happen.

The DHSS summary also emphasized that tragedies seemed to occur when there was inadequate record-keeping and a failure to set explicit plans of action or to review any plan in a systematic way. The section of the summary on professional practice con-cluded: 'Effective communication and records are integral to good practice. Inadequate professional responses often stem from communicating and recording inaccurately or not at all, from failing to tap sources of information instead of "waiting to be told" and from recording information in ways which make it difficult to use or collate.'

All these points relate to efficient management and organ-ization, an area, presumably, that would be relatively easy to reform, and have little to do with the broader theories of contemporary social work. Even so, five years after the DHSS *Review of Child Abuse Cases* the Beckford report attacked precisely these same points again. Although it is known that individual local authorities which have been subjected to official inquiries have changed their practices in response to specific criticisms directed at them, basic recommendations made time and again which could be universally applied seem to have been largely ignored by the majority of social workers who have not been involved in a personal tragedy themselves.

The most hopeful recent development since the Beckford inquiry has been the announcement of a national policy on the management of child abuse by the British Association of Social Workers which this organization wants to see adopted by every local authority. The professional body took two years to produce the policy statement, which includes detailed codes of practice, and in his introduction the chairman of the project admits that it was difficult for those considering the guidelines to agree on what should be said. 'This points', he says, 'to the major difficulties practitioners have in feeling confident about their policies, procedures and practices in such an emotive environment.' In spite of these misgivings, however, the codes of procedure are clear and direct and stress that the child should always be considered the primary client in any abusing family, that social workers responsible for child-abuse cases should have had specific post-qualification training, and that crucial decisions about the management of children at risk should be taken only on the basis of multi-disciplinary expert advice. If all local authorities adopt the new policy, and social workers become more responsive to the ideas of their own professional leadership than they have been to the suggestions of external authorities who have written inquiry reports, then there is some hope that in future at least the most glaring administrative mistakes will be avoided.

Even so, many of the more subtle problems of assessing the risks in different family circumstances will probably remain untouched. As long as maintaining and rehabilitating the natural family remains the primary goal of social work there will still be acute difficulties in balancing the fear that a child will be abused against the fear that a family will be broken. In the past a combination of factors seems to have made all of us, professionals and lay public, over-optimistic about the number of children at high risk in their own homes. Public opinion has been too disturbed by the implications of recognizing the extent and nature of child abuse to do more than react with ephemeral indignation to what have been seen as random scandals. Social workers have fought shy of what they see as unwarranted intrusion into their professional world by external critics and uninformed, hysterical commentators, and have almost deliberately failed to accept the lessons of their own colleagues' mistakes. Parents have reacted with instinctive hostility to the idea that their children's best interests may be judged by experts, who in turn may censure parental behaviour and care. The idea of distinguishing the rights of a child from the rights of the parents is still threatening and alien to many people. It is time to look more courageously and honestly at what is happening to those children who are battered, or physically or emotionally deprived or sexually assaulted, and to be flexibly pragmatic in our efforts to deal with them. We must make it impossible for any child in the future to plead for death as four-year-old Kimberley Carlile was reported to have done after months of torture in a London suburb in the mid-1980s.

# 2   FAMILY TIES

Keeping families together and supervising the family unit is not an easy job. Most of the children who have been injured come from families that are fraught with all sorts of problems, which makes it difficult for the members of those families to deal with the day-to-day routine. Each additional problem may compound the last until someone erupts in violence. Some families have been on the social services files for generations, spawning new, complicated branches with their own often disturbed, inadequate or violent backgrounds. So it is immensely complicated to assess the risks and judge any progress. The social worker who enters the family makes contact with the parents and strives to maintain a good relationship with them as they provide access to the child and the hope for the child's future. As a result the parents, rather than their beleaguered children, too often become the focus of attention.

Children are often sent back home even where there is considerable risk, and what is called a 'distinct lack of parenting abilities'. A major dilemma for most social services departments is how much aid and support they should go on pumping into one particular family in order to keep them together, rather than simply pulling out some of the support, allowing the family to deteriorate and then removing the child. It is not an easy decision. But it is not made easier by focusing on the family needs rather than on the needs of a particular child.

Children who are known to have been abused are often put on a care order, and the local authority then becomes their legal parent. Sometimes they are removed and sent to temporary foster-homes, where they will stay until it is considered safe to send them home or 'rehabilitate' them. There are no clear definitions of 'safe' and practice varies from authority to authority, but children who are rehabilitated, or who stay with their families once they are known to have been abused, are put on an 'at-risk register' and everyone who formally comes into contact with the family, such as health visitors, doctors, or teachers, is informed. Families with children on the register are given high priority. There are frequent visits, the family is supervised and monitored at great expense, and much attention is paid to any bruises, cuts or accidents. The cases are reviewed regularly both at local level and by the area review committee.

Rehabilitation is considered good social-work practice. Social workers are critical of the rash of fostering which follows inquiries such as the Colwell and Beckford cases because they feel it is done to protect the social workers themselves rather than the children. They are fully aware of the risk in sending children home once they have been injured, but they feel that this has to be balanced against the emotional damage children suffer away from their real family. They are also sensitive to parents' needs and are prepared to give families a second chance – if they think the parents are willing to improve. Social workers believe – and their training encourages them to think – that they can change people from being bad or indifferent parents to adequate or at least non-violent parents.

There is a risk in sending any child home, even if the monitoring is impeccable. It takes only seconds to kill a child and no one can supervise a family for twenty-four hours a day. The difficulty lies in trying to separate the children who are very high risk from those less at risk. Differentiating between the two is crucial, and may make the difference between death and saving a life. Sometimes children are reunited with parents who can barely cope and who have to be supervised and slowly taught how to be better parents. In some families the amount of support is enormous; there may be daily home help, family aides, nursery places and regular health-visitor and social-work visits. If any one of those supports disappears too soon the family might well resort to violence, so continuous and accurate assessment is vital and depends on pooling medical and social information. The overall responsibility lies with the social services department, and their judgement is crucial. They know they take a risk, but feel they can calculate it fairly accurately. No one knows how accurate they are until something goes wrong, and then the calculation appears all too inexact – particularly when it is based on the interests of the family rather than those of the child.

Belief in the natural family is fully endorsed by the courts. The magistrate in the case of Jasmine Beckford recommended that she should be returned to her family as soon as possible. This confirmed the social workers' strong preference and Jasmine was in fact sent back to her home, even though she had been violently assaulted and her stepfather was known to have had an extremely brutal upbringing himself.

Jasmine lived with her mother Beverley Lorrington, her step-father Morris Beckford and her stepsister Louise in a dilapidated flat in north London. When she was twenty months old she was admitted to hospital with a fracture to her leg. The doctors were convinced that it was due to rough treatment and was non-accidental. Both she and her sister were put into a foster-home.

Her mother and Morris Beckford very much wanted the girls back. It had been noted that the parents had paid little attention to the children in hospital, and the mother in particular had no idea how to talk to or play with her children. Jasmine seemed to have no relationship with her mother, and when she was two she befriended anyone who showed her any affection, which is unusual in a child of that age. She was also underweight, but when she left the hospital and went to foster-parents she thrived. A programme was devised for the Beckfords to learn how to look after their children properly, so that the girls could return to them and develop normally. Morris and Beverley visited the girls at a nursery, and were shown by the staff how to play with their children, how to talk to them, how to help them develop. They seemed good learners and progressed to having the children home with them occasionally. Finally the little girls were sent home, despite the protests of the foster-parents, who felt they would be at considerable risk.

So after seven months the family were reunited and moved into a newly decorated three-bedroomed council house. The rehabilitation programme continued. A family aide came in regularly, often three times a week, to show them how to play, what to cook, how to clean most efficiently. The social worker popped in continuously to chat about any problems, and a health visitor called in occasionally. Everyone agreed that the improvements were startling. Social workers became less concerned, and fewer visits were made. The girls were rarely seen and then one day the unthinkable happened. Jasmine was killed.

In fact her death had been slow. She had not been seen by anyone for three months before her death and had suffered terrible injuries during that time. The social workers found the tragedy difficult to accept. They had few doubts that they had been right to send Jasmine back to her parents. The inquiry held after her death concluded that they had never kept the child's interest paramount, but had been distracted by the demands of the parents. They had not seen Jasmine enough, or been sufficiently concerned about her physical or educational progress. They had been seduced by their relationship with the parents into thinking that the child was not at risk.

When the public roared its disapproval in the newspaper headlines, the social-work profession felt under siege. It was convenient for them to distance themselves from the practice in the London borough where Jasmine had died. Elsewhere, they told themselves, judgements were more cautious, practice more assiduous, rehabilitation more meticulously managed. Other departments reflected that if such a tragedy were to happen on their doorstep they could at least claim that they had done everything that should have been done.

The assumption behind all this was that if all the errors in supervision could be ironed out there would be no more cases such as this – or at least far fewer. But after nineteen inquiries, all advocating the same vigilance, that assumption is scarcely realistic. Even if everything were carried out according to the books, rehabilitation is an immensely high-risk practice.

To find out how such risks are calculated, and the child monitored if he or she is sent home, we visited a large social services department. We told the department that we wanted a case which was receiving a great deal of attention, where the family was being supported in every possible way and where everything was being done according to the book (so the social workers could not be faulted) but where the child was still very much at risk. We were keen to see good social-work practice, and the department very kindly co-operated with us. They offered us a very dramatic case which, despite their careful monitoring, had ended in tragedy. When we arrived at the department it occupied the attention of a social worker almost full time and also pre-occupied her senior. The social-work team were confident they had not made mistakes. They had endlessly pored over the files of notes, had visited very frequently, had put in a great deal of continuous support and had made the correct line-management decisions. Following hard on the Beckford inquiry they had made sure that none of the professional errors which had cost Jasmine her life could happen in their team.

In particular the social workers adapted their practice to take account of the central criticism in the Beckford case. That report had taken the social worker (Gun Wahlstrom) to task for being preoccupied with the parents and losing sight of the child who was legally in her care. Wahlstrom believed that, as her relation-ship with the parents improved and grew more open and trust-ing, it would be reflected in their handling of Jasmine. Her reports were very much taken up with the adults' problems. She had expected that the family aide would give practical help and that the health visitor would pick up any physical problems. However, because her relationship with the parents improved, and Morris Beckford, who had initially been hostile, grew to accept her, she was lulled into a false sense of security. She felt that the parents should be allowed to live their own lives and be trusted, once they had had a trial period. Both she and her senior were convinced they would not harm Jasmine again. They thought the original fracture was a 'one-off explosion', and were optimistic about their own work with the family, which had brought about considerable improvements. They believed that the Beckfords had fundamentally changed for the better.

One of the conclusions of the Beckford inquiry was that the social worker should never have lost sight of the real client – the child. It was the child and not the parents who was in the care of the social services department. The report concluded, 'To treat the parents as the clients is fatally to misdirect the efforts of what is in essence a child protection service,' adding, 'We fear that their attitude in regarding the parents of children in care as the clients rather than the children in their own right may be widespread among social workers.'

To avoid this particular mistake the department we visited appointed two social workers, one for the parents and one for the child. The workers visited together, to make sure that one of them was free to concentrate on the child while the other talked to the mother. Even so, the case went horribly wrong. In a way we had never planned, it pinpointed the weakness in the rehabilitation process.

Alia Aziz first came to the attention of the north area team in a city borough when she was one year old. She was admitted to hospital with seven fractures, some of them going back over a period of eight weeks. Her body was covered with bruises: there was a bite mark on her calf and pinpricks on the soles of her feet. The paediatrician was in no doubt that the child had been badly battered. The parents denied this vociferously and tried to account for all the various marks and breakages. None of the explanations satisfied the social workers or the doctors. While in hospital readings were taken of Alia's relationship with her parents. The hospital noticed that the child withdrew from the mother and sat rocking a lot, and that the mother did not pick her up. The child was sent to a foster-parent.

Alia stayed there for just a month. During that time the social worker took over. She visited the parents, who were Kenyan Asians, and was impressed by their spotlessly clean home (despite being in a run-down area) and their anxiety about their daughter. The parents visited the foster-home every day. The child was a twin and had been briefly adopted when she was born, but had gone back to live at home when she was just over three months old because the couple who had adopted her were expecting their own baby. Her parents had lost a great deal of face in the local Asian community by taking the child back and were consequently quite isolated. They overwhelmed the social workers and the foster-parents alike with their sense of guilt and their desire above all else to have their little girl returned. After four weeks the social workers, impressed with the loving, concerned attitude of the mother and finding absolutely no evidence that she had ill-treated her daughter, thought the child should be sent home. The department understood that there was a considerable risk, particularly because the mother was expecting a baby imminently. Alia had one elder sister beside her twin, so that meant there would be four children under four years old at home. But they decided that, with a visit from a family aide five times a week and a nursery place for the eldest child, Alia and her twin would be safe.

That was clearly the first mistake. Within six weeks Alia was back in hospital, this time with a major head injury which resulted in retinal haemorrhages. The doctors agreed that it had been caused by very violent shaking. They were concerned that she might be permanently brain-damaged.

This time she was sent to a foster-home, with no plan for her to return to her parents. That was in January 1984. Alia was fourteen months old. She blossomed in the foster-home and made rapid strides in her development. Her parents saw her often and still offered no explanation of how she had come by her injuries. The social worker looking after the family found them overwhelmed by grief at not having their child back and at the same time they were absolutely insistent that they had not injured her.

After six months in the foster-home, the social services department sent a letter to Alia's parents saying she would not be returning home as they were clearly unable to look after her properly or account for her injuries. The effect was dramatic. The father almost immediately confessed to having injured the child, and talks began about the possibility of returning Alia. Amazingly, three months later the department had drawn up a rehabilitation agreement. After another three months Alia was allowed to return home. That was in January 1985. She had been in the foster-home for a year, and was now two years old. Her father had left and there was talk of divorce.

Both the rehabilitation and the return home were deemed successful. She appeared to have flourished. Everything seemed to go well during the next year. Alia had her third birthday. Then, three months later, in March 1986, she was taken to hospital with a bleeding and enormously swollen head. The paediatrician diagnosed a heavy blow to the head.

At this point it would be all too easy to throw up one's hands in horror and dwell on the endemic incompetence of social workers who clearly never learn. That would be a normal reaction to such a painful story. But it is crucial to bear in mind that this was considered by the team to be good social work. The team in question tend to deal mainly with children, although they have no specialized training. All of them are very experienced social workers who have been on a number of child-abuse courses and have dealt with many children at risk. They are hard-working and enthusiastic, and extremely concerned about their clients, recording all their visits meticulously.

To understand why the case nonetheless went tragically wrong, it has to be understood why the social workers decided to send one-year-old Alia home for the second time, six months after the department had written to her parents to say there was no chance of her returning home. What had happened in those six months was critical for the social workers. There had been, in their rather graphic language, a 'disclosure', which in lay terms meant a confession. Mr Aziz had admitted to the injuries. To the social workers that meant the possibility of a new relationship, built on honesty and trust. When the natural parents were told in no uncertain terms that they were not going to have Alia back because there was no explanation of how she had received her injuries, it dawned on them that they could get Alia back if they confessed. Within a month the father admitted mistreating the child, twisting her limbs until he heard the bones click. He accounted for all the injuries except for the violent shaking, which remained a mystery.

The senior social worker told us that the social services department was 'in all cases duty-bound to consider the potential for rehabilitation and to see whether the child's needs could be met in her own family'. So sending Alia home was very much at the back of the team's minds all along. The social worker, Lisette Burton, explained: 'When I first took over the case I thought to myself there is no way that I will ever return that child who has had seven fractures to her mother. Then I got to know the mother and she overwhelmed me with her desire to have her child back. She was like a lioness in the way she protected her children. And when they opened up to us and told us what had happened I saw that we could actually work with them. We all felt we had the measure of them.' To this her senior added crucially, 'We felt we could safeguard the child against further harm and help the family therapeutically. We hoped to bring about change and you cannot do that unless you engage the family and understand their pressures. We knew what they had done; we knew about their financial difficulties. They told us about their domestic problems. Once you have established that relationship of trust you can work with them.'

After the 'disclosure' the case took on a different complexion. No one seemed too concerned that the mother had clearly known about the violence to the child and, perhaps, had even been a party to it. Suddenly there was the possibility of change. The parents had opened up. The social workers could work with them now. This, combined with the overwhelming desire of the mother to get her child back, led the social workers to prepare a programme for the return of little Alia for the second time.

Jasmine Beckford's parents had desperately wanted her back too. They had insisted that they could look after both Jasmine and her sister Louise. No one had been particularly happy with the parenting abilities of Jasmine's mother. In the early days, when she was at the hospital and visiting Jasmine at the foster-parents', several experts had commented on the fact that she could not talk to the children and did not know how to play with them. But once the family aide was sent in to show her how to talk to the children and play with them, things improved rapidly. Everyone was delighted with the progress. The past was forgotten.

By contrast no one had been worried about Alia's mother. The hospital staff had noticed that the child had been wary of her, but no one else seemed to have noticed this. The reports are most sympathetic. The mother had visited the child regularly. She seemed to understand the predicament and the difficulties her daughter faced with the foster-parents. She phoned the social workers every day. Unlike a great many of the mothers the department dealt with, Mrs Aziz was over-anxious and quite desperate to have her child back. Even before the 'disclosure' they thought of her as genuine and her grief over the loss of her daughter utterly believable. The problem was that the overpowering presence of the mother blinded them to the child.

When Mrs Aziz had been told that rehabilitation had become a possibility she could barely contain her excitement. Although the original idea had been couched in cautious language, and discussed as a long-term project with fairly intensive supervision, the mother hardly took this on board. An agreement was drawn up which had as its goal 'the successful rehabilitation of Alia with her parents', so clearly the social workers were feeling quite optimistic.

Alia was reintegrated into her family slowly and carefully. The programme was based on the peculiarly social-work notion of 'trust'. All the adults had to trust each other and be open and honest about their problems. This meant that, although Alia's parents were having an extremely difficult time with each other, and the household was desperately short of money, as long as it could be talked about it could be dealt with. And talk about it to the social services visitors the parents constantly did. Over all this period Alia's visits home were carefully watched. The foster-parents were asked for their reaction when she returned home. Health visitors made sure that clinics were attended. The family aide was there to see that Mrs Aziz could cope with her domestic organization. The family was caressed, nurtured and cosseted. The father, who had appeared to be at the root of the problem, had moved away, and was not allowed to see his daughter on his own. At the end of the trial period, the social workers could write quite confidently that the father would not harm any of the children now that the previous history of violence was out in the open. The health visitor concurred. So did the foster-parents and the family aide. The child went home.

Clearly the social workers thought that everything had changed, just as the social workers had with the Beckfords. And yet even before Alia went home there were ominous signs. Once after a visit she had returned to her foster-parents with a cut lip. This was followed by a visit of three social workers who demanded an explanation. The father claimed that she had cut her lip when he pulled a toy from her mouth. They went away satisfied. Two other bruises were carefully noted. No doctor was called on these occasions, because the local GP had at all times refused to co-operate with the social services department. The general view was that Alia was fit and well and extremely well integrated with her family. The trust in the family and the mother's apparent openness made the social workers feel reasonably confident that Alia would be quite safe at home and that that was the best place for her. Her rehabilitation took three months.

To underline the steps taken to ensure Alia's safety once she had returned home, Lisette listed for the record the 'input': there was a joint social-work visit weekly and an ethnic-minority worker visit weekly, two family aides called once a week, a free place was provided for the eldest child in nursery school as well as nursery places for Alia and her twin to start immediately. The health visitor was programmed. The cost of supporting that one family ran into hundreds of pounds a week. No one who visited the home and dealt with the mother had anything but praise for the way she was coping.

Unlike the Beckford case, the vigilance did not cease. When Jasmine Beckford went to nursery, the social worker thought she should have a clean start. To show her trust in the mother, she decided not to tell the nursery that Jasmine was on the at-risk register nor to reveal anything about her history. So the nursery teachers were not alerted to any possible dangers. The social workers we visited made no such mistakes. They had proper management of the case and had no intention of taking the child off the register. The nursery was given full information on the two-year-old, so when they saw the first sign of bruising they immediately spoke to the mother and the social workers. They told the social workers that the mother had not given them an adequate explanation for all the little cuts and bruises the child seemed to have on her face, and they were not happy with the way the child behaved. They felt she was afraid of her mother, and they were worried that she could not settle down and seemed very aggressive.

The social workers immediately took action. The mother was angry that her word had been doubted by the nursery teachers. She listed in great detail the places where Alia had received the bruises and cuts. She even took Lisette down a road to show her the exact stones on which she claimed Alia had stumbled. 'It was not', recorded Lisette, 'the sort of spot I would have chosen if I had been lying.' Lisette then decided to observe the child at the nursery, but the mother did not take the twins for the next few days, and the social worker could not find her. She eventually tracked her down via the family's solicitor, only to discover that the husband had returned, forced himself on the mother, and hit Alia. There was more panic and more social workers went back to the house, where they did indeed notice three definite finger-marks on Alia's arms. By then the father had left. The social workers impressed on the mother how important it was to let them know if she were going away or if anything happened. But they felt enough confidence in the mother, the protective lioness, not to take the child to the doctor. They left reassured.

The twins went to the nursery for the next ten days, then the teacher noticed another small bruise on Alia and challenged the mother. At once she stopped taking the twins. The nursery phoned the social workers. Discussions ensued. The mother felt threatened by the nursery teachers, who wanted explanations for every mark they saw. The social workers sympathized with the mother and felt that the nursery was being over-attentive. The team leader explained that it was very difficult being under continuous pressure and that the mother had found it too much. Far from seeing the nursery as doing an effective monitoring job, the senior social worker claimed that 'The nursery staff were only doing their job. They were not to know how much pressure they were putting on Mrs Aziz and how difficult it was for her to deal with that.' Additionally it appeared that Alia's behaviour had deteriorated markedly at the nursery; she had started soiling and had become very aggressive. The social workers formally closed the nursery places making sure that there was other monitoring. They were not inclined to listen to the nursery teachers' reports. Instead they scheduled Alia and her twin to report every fortnight to the clinic and made elaborate transport arrangements with taxi firms. They did not check with the health visitor, assuming that if anything had been amiss they would have been informed. They also tended to dismiss many of the health visitor's doubts expressed at meetings. She had reported that the family was very secretive and seemed to be hiding something, but she could not be sure. At one point she had also ventured that the parents might be abusing the twins, although in the face of the general optimism about the family that was a difficult claim to sustain. At the same time the health visitor never commented on the many bruises the child had suffered. There was no contact at all with the local GP, who never came to case conferences although invited. The confidence of the social workers and family aides remained undiminished.

It is difficult to distinguish the roles of the two social workers allotted to the family. Their briefs may have been different, but their reports are remarkably similar. The social worker for the child never actually saw Alia on her own. She wanted Alia to feel integrated with her family and not set apart. She felt she had been separated enough and was at pains not to give her special attention, so she treated her exactly as she did the other children. She was conscious that the mother did not want her to have any physical contact with her daughter. She never took Alia out alone as she felt she was too small and would have been anxious away from her mother. Nor did she ever really speak to Alia, as the child knew hardly any English and the few words she had learned were in Punjabi. She did note at one point that her speech was improving as she was able to gabble back quite fluently to her mother. But presumably she had no means of knowing whether the child was talking properly. But Alia was watched. It was noted that she was a lively, playful little girl who seemed affectionate but was often left out. She appeared to have been picked on by the mother, who found her difficult, although the social workers found her twin far more aggressive. All this was noted, but because neither social worker was a child-care specialist it was absorbed into an overall family picture.

It is the mother who dominated the reports and elicited the compassion and sympathy of her myriad helpers. She bombarded the workers with her problems, which appear to have been endless. There were marital problems; she separated; she considered divorce; she denied access; she castigated her lazy husband, but then again she allowed him to pop in and out. She was ambivalent about marriage and about her husband. Then there were financial problems. She never had enough to live on. She managed with four small children on £20 a week. Her husband was unreliable. A great deal of time was spent sorting out her various benefits, arranging an extra grant for her, getting people in to clear the garden, organizing the taxis to the clinic. Then there were family problems: because she had separated she had become even more cut off from her family and the community. Sometimes she was conciliatory; at other times belligerent and resentful of all the pressure on her from the

helpers as well as from the children. On one occasion she told
Lisette that she was reluctant to let the children get too close to
her because she did not want them to turn out like white women,
casual in relation to men.

Through all this the social workers never doubted that she
was a good mother. The children were always well fed, in
fact overfed, and beautifully turned out. The house was
always clean. The girls seemed to play happily and there seemed to be an immense bond between the children and their
mother, which everyone noted – the health visitor, social
workers and family aides.

The mother managed to exhaust both social workers.
Although one of them was supposed to concentrate on the
children and the other to deal with her, in fact her nervous
energy consumed them both. Her list of complaints and demands
was endless. She needed the social workers and resented them.
Usually the social workers accepted her requests in order to get
some peace. They even let her take her children out of the
nursery school to ease her life. They took the mother's side
against the nursery school, and concurred that the nursery
school staff were perhaps being too insensitive and interfering,
when clearly they were merely doing their job rather well.
Interestingly the nursery staff focused on the child and not on
the mother and saw things the social workers missed. There was
unfortunately no medical feedback as the local GP consistently
refused to contact the social workers. But Alia did go to the
clinic.

On her first visit to the clinic Alia had a bruise on her lip.
The mother explained that this was because of a fall and the
health visitor, who had known the family for some time,
accepted this explanation. On the next visit she noticed that
Alia walked with a limp and she insisted that the child be taken
to hospital. The mother became belligerent about this, but
ultimately agreed to go. Everything had gone according to the
book so far. The paediatrician examined the child and concluded
that the injury was accidental. He accepted the mother's explanation. The social workers' fears had been allayed. No one
could say whether the child's notes had been checked.

A series of other bruises followed. All were seen at the clinic,
and in each case the stories appear to have been accepted as

plausible. Alia seems to have chalked up a rather large number of accidents and bruises for a two-and-a-half-year-old. Yet curiously, when a review of her case was held in September 1985 after she had been home for nine months it was noted that 'there had been no injuries since access had begun'. The bruising had been overshadowed by her progress. She had been to the clinic every two weeks and had gained weight. She had begun to talk, and she had a reasonably good relationship with her sisters and her mother. The social worker had even scored the mother and child behaviour on the Vera Hardberg scale, for eye contact, bonding and so on, and they had come out very high. After nearly a year at home the level of support was still astonishing but it was considered absolutely necessary.

From September 1985 until the following March, when three-year-old Alia was brought into hospital, bruises continued to appear, some of them quite severe. At times the mother volunteered information about them spontaneously, which the social workers found most encouraging. On one occasion Lisette noted that she would never have seen the cut inside Alia's lip if the mother had not pointed it out. This reinforced her notion of trust with the mother.

But two of the injuries sound far more serious. Towards the end of 1985, after Alia had been a year at home, Lisette noticed a large bruise on her forehead. The mother claimed she had fallen down the stairs, Alia did not seem to be any the worse for wear, and the social worker felt happy with her condition. It appeared that Alia was affectionate towards her mother, and the notes record 'no signs of uneasiness'. One month later when the social workers visited they noticed that the child had a lump on her head and a black eye. The mother explained that Alia, then aged three, had climbed on to a chair and toppled into the china cabinet. She was rushed to hospital and there she was x-rayed. But that revealed nothing, and no one saw any danger.

Around the turn of the year the mother complained bitterly about being under pressure. That was partly due, or so she would have had everyone believe, to the swarms of helpers who attended her at home and watched her constantly. She took up again with her husband and began to insist that he had never harmed his daughter. Money problems continued to aggravate her. Much of the resentment was directed towards the hapless Alia. The mother fought against having to go to the clinic, although the social workers insisted. She said she did not need family aides. Her children seemed to be constantly sick. They were taken to the local GP fourteen times in January to March 1986. The stress was clearly beginning to tell, although as late as February Alia was reported to be 'in good form'.

Then the inevitable happened. The mother's story was that the child had fallen on her chin and her head had swollen. She had taken the child to the doctor who, in turn, had sent her off to the hospital. The hospital had discharged Alia that same night. The social workers, on a routine visit, took one look at her and were so horrified by her gigantically bloated head that they took her straight back to the hospital and made the doctor examine her more closely and check her notes. The paediatrician diagnosed a deliberate blow to the head. The social workers were stunned and sought a second opinion, which confirmed the first. Six months later they were still unable to understand what had happened; they felt it was inconceivable that she had been battered.

The social workers' conclusions were that the hospital had diagnosed on the basis of the child's previous history, without having had the benefit of witnessing her happy relationship with her mother or of observing her general improvement. We asked what mistakes they thought they had made in the case, given what had happened. Lisette replied: 'I suppose if she has really been injured as they say then we should never have rehabilitated her in the first place. That was the mistake.'

The Beckford report, *A Child in Trust*, had this to say in one of its concluding paragraphs:

> Dr Kempe, the author of the concept, the battered-child syndrome, once wrote: 'if a child is not safe at home, he cannot be protected by case work' ... nothing that we have heard at our Inquiry or read in the reports of other inquiries and in the various studies and research findings detracts one iota from the profound wisdom of that statement.

In the Aziz case the social workers felt that the risks were high, but that they could still protect the child and support the family.

The Beckford report argued for better procedures and for

better liaison between doctors, social workers and teachers. These were quite well followed in the Aziz case. The social services department adopted a fairly dismissive attitude towards doctors and health visitors, but still they were consulted. Certainly the medical profession never raised the alarm – not even the clinic. The mistake was to think that the child should or could be returned home, to ignore anything that did not fit into that picture and to be lulled into a state of optimism about change. The idea that you can turn completely unsafe parents into safer parents, and bad into good, with a short-term, massive input of workers is fairly unrealistic. Change of this order of magnitude involves very long-term therapy. In the Aziz case, as in the Beckford, had there been change it would most probably have come much too late.

Social workers believe, and are taught to believe, that change is possible. Indeed it is difficult to work for weeks and months with someone and not see any improvements. Their clients are nearly always those under great stress, the most deprived. They are people who live in the worst housing conditions, with the poorest education and the least disposable income. Yet social workers are supposed to work some magic with such people. You cannot, however, unpick the habits of a lifetime in a short period. The more cruel, vicious or inadequate, the more the work. Often because the work with the clients is very personal, and the assessments subjective, change is difficult to measure. It is the result of an intuitive assessment, of instinct and experience.

When we described their clients in this way to the social workers they were horrified at our lack of sympathy. Social workers are trained to be non-judgemental and tolerant, and these are without doubt essential qualities for the work they do. But these very qualities also blind them not a little to the mammoth task they set themselves. Although Lisette and her senior had been quite shocked at our description of their clients, they did agree that it was probably correct. In the last few years Lisette's cases have become considerably worse. Currently she has seventeen, all of which concern abused or badly neglected children. They are often sent to school filthy, smelly and underfed. They are frequently either withdrawn or over-aggressive. Some do not talk very fluently. Most of them live in poor housing in bleak council estates. In such an environment, Lisette expects to find abuse.

The Aziz family did not fit into this mould. Their house was always spotless. The children were all beautifully dressed and clean. The mother played with her small children on the floor, or sat and read them stories. The children were overfed and overweight, ebullient and extrovert. Over the weeks and months Alia appeared to develop normally. At two and a half she was sent to the hospital for a check-up and her progress was considered to be normal. And so the social workers began to treat her and the family as normal. But no child who has had seven fractures and a brain haemorrhage could be considered normal – and that was the fatal mistake.

Observations were put into a normal setting. The nursery school supervisors who insisted that the explanation for the cuts and bruises were inadequate were thought to be over-fussy. Other bruises were too readily accepted as having been acquired in an ordinary way. Even when the father had slapped Alia hard on the arm and left clear marks, the mother was only given a warning. After nine months at home, the case-review claimed that Alia had not been injured since access. All her injuries had been defined as accidental, and neither the clinic nor the hospital had set any alarm bells ringing. However good the procedures, they are only as good as the people who carry them out. In this case neither the medical staff nor the social workers saw very much cause for concern.

The pattern was set. After nine months it appeared that this apparently happy little girl was safe. Social workers trusted the mother, and were convinced that she would protect the children against the father, although she had singularly failed to do this in the past. They allowed she was 'heavy-handed' at times, but she was certainly no worse than other mothers on their patch. They had no reason to doubt their own eyes ... except, of course, as regards the early history. But that had long since faded. She had been classified as a good mother and the social workers were inextricably entangled in her day-to-day practical problems. Although there was a special worker designated for Alia she did not get special attention. The child's social worker was not trained differently from the other social worker who visited. She was there to double up with her colleague, reduce the stress and provide a separate set of observations. None of the workers who saw the family in the eighteen-month period saw any danger signs. The increasing number of bruises were all written off as the unfortunate accidents of a child who was not very stable on her feet.

No one ever did a psychiatric assessment on the parents, although there were suggestions from the health visitor at the various conferences that the mother in particular seemed disturbed. No one had checked further back than the parents' marriage. Yet it is well known that people who are battered themselves become battering parents. That was certainly the case with Morris Beckford.

Despite Alia's inordinately high number of cuts, bruises and scratches the social workers readily accepted the mother's explanation for them. They believed they had formed a 'trusting relationship' and were not prepared to doubt that judgement. Yet it was abundantly clear that the mother had covered up for the husband for a long time. And it was conceivable that she had lied about some of the bruises. Although Lisette and her colleagues would doubtless be horrified at the comparison, the conclusions in the Beckford inquiry report could be our own. There it was noted that the principles of a

> 'non-judgemental' attitude ... instilled in social-work
> students are entirely appropriate for case-work with adults.
> But such an approach can be disastrous if applied to parents
> caring for children they have seriously abused.... Both
> social worker and her supervising senior went along with the
> parents' earnest desire to have their children back home....
> they were only too willing to accept the parents' explanations
> for the absence of the children from home when visits were
> made, reflected in the maddening phrase of Ms Wahlstrom
> that 'she had no reason to disbelieve' the explanations....

Lisette and her team saw no reason to disbelieve Mrs Aziz. They were firmly committed to their own observations, which centred on how well the mother was relating to the children, and the children to the mother, and they convinced themselves that further abuse was impossible. The mother must undoubtedly have been warm and physical, but she was also clearly violent and unpredictable. The social worker's judgements were based on the quality of family life. They never saw Alia's growth chart, and they never checked her speech. They were not child specialists.

In fact, they observed but did not see, and they listened but did not hear. Little Alia is now with foster-parents. She is severely retarded, mentally and physically, and very disturbed.

Not all children who are sent back to their families end up like Jasmine and Alia. In high-risk cases there is generally a massive investment in social-work time and resources. But the definition of 'high risk' seems to differ widely. In one social services department we visited in the Midlands we met a high-risk family where the abuse was quite mild in comparison to the abuse Alia had suffered but where the concern was, if anything, greater. Rehabilitation was cautious, and there were grave doubts about whether it would succeed. But once the nine-week rehabilitation period was over, even though there were distinct problems, the family remained together.

Don Atkinson had badly beaten his two stepchildren, who had been seen at school with belt-marks across their backs and bad bruising. Both Don and his wife had been known to social services for some time as his 'child-care abilities were not very high'. Visits to the home revealed unbelievable squalor: buckets of urine dotted about, piles of unwashed clothes scattered everywhere. The children were often locked in their rooms for long periods and neighbours had frequently complained about their treatment. The mother had been married before and had had three children. One of them had been killed by her husband, who had been jailed as a result. She set up house with Don and had two more children, in whom she seemed totally uninterested.

Once the belt-marks were discovered, all four children were put into a foster-home. The elder two, who had clearly been beaten, were put into a long-term home. But Don wanted to keep the younger two with him. He split up from his overweight, sluttish wife and moved into his parents' home. There, under his parents' supervision, he begged to be allowed to have the children back. He promised to give up his job so that he could devote all his time to the children and give them the care they needed. The social services department relented and offered him a nine-week test programme with family aides, nursery places for the two children, calls from a health visitor and weekly social-worker visits. They felt that with the grandparents in the house the children would be protected. They made it clear that after nine weeks they would review his progress, and if his handling of the children had not improved they would be taken back to the foster-home.

It was not an easy nine weeks for anybody. The social workers had to teach Don from scratch. He had to learn not to let the children play with plugs and climb over him when he had a cigarette. A daily family aide patiently took toys out of a box every day in the hope that both Don and his small children would learn how to play together. The children were given a place at nursery and Don was required to go to the nursery regularly and take part. The social worker visited several times a week and all the helpers met at regular intervals to discuss the case. After nine weeks they still felt frustrated. Don did not seem to understand how to sit and eat calmly at the nursery. He could not talk calmly to the children but seemed always to overexcite them; when he played with them his interest wandered. The family aide who came in daily scored him regularly on a test she had devised which checked whether he had left the handles of pots on the cooker within easy reach of the children, whether he let them climb into the oven, how often he actually played with them, and so on. His score was erratic. After six weeks on the programme the department had pulled out all the support and within a day Don had reverted to his former self: the children were unkempt, poorly fed and sitting all day in front of the TV. Once the support had returned, however, he slowly remembered what he was supposed to do.

After the nine-week test period Don had learned some things but clearly could not be trusted on his own. The children were beginning to have problems. The four-year-old was being seen by a speech therapist because her talking had deteriorated. She had frequent temper tantrums. The five-year-old boy was sleeping badly and becoming difficult to control. They did not seem to be making progress with their father. But he was desperate to keep them and they clearly had a great deal of affection for him. So another two months of close supervision and observation was planned in the hope that one day Don would be able to cope by himself with his two children. As we left after our visit to the department, the social worker muttered, 'I wish we had the guts to pull out now.'

And that must remain the central dilemma for the social services: how long can they continue to shore up families like Don's before they give up? If they pull out any of the supports the risks become very high. It is not simply a question of balancing costs. The money spent on family aide, nursery school, social worker and health visitor is probably no greater than the cost of keeping a child in a foster-home. It is much more a question of calculating the risks to the child of being battered or damaged, compared to the safety of a foster-home.

Don had never beaten the two smaller children, although he had been quite brutal with the older two. And no one was allowed to forget that. Josh Cooper, the young, rather fashionable social worker who had learned about child abuse on the job, was under no illusion about his own therapeutic relationship with Don. He was friendly, but fairly authoritative. When we first visited Don at home we were touched by the father's warm and loving relationship with his little girl. When she cried he picked her up and nestled her into his lap and gently kissed her. He took her into the kitchen to pick out a mug. He emptied the toy box on to the floor for her to play with. He looked like the model father. But the family aide and nursery teacher spelled out the list of omissions. He clearly would not pass an MOT in fathering. For a brief moment the scrutiny seemed unfair, until we remembered the background.

# 3    THE LETHAL FAMILY

The Beckford inquiry had been making its painful way through
the details of Jasmine's short life for several weeks when two
experts appeared and gave evidence which both educated and
exasperated the listeners. Professor Cyril Greenland and Dr
Leonard Taitz gave their separate opinions that it was possible
to draw up a profile of families whose children might be in
danger and that, once danger was suspected, there were good,
objective ways of assessing the children which should make it
impossible to hide abuse and neglect. In other words, the tools
exist to identify and monitor high-risk families. The confused
subjectivity of personal impressions, coloured by false optimism,
which had guided the management of the Beckford family, and
which guides a great deal of social-work practice, is simply
inappropriate. It could be replaced, or at least greatly streng-
thened, by a form of analysis which has been available for some
time, but is just not used by social services departments, who
have the primary responsibility for child-abuse cases. The evidence suggested that Jasmine Beckford, and other children like
her, might not have died if this analysis had been used: it was
not surprising that many who heard this were very angry.

Professor Cyril Greenland is an English academic who has
enormous experience of child abuse on both sides of the Atlan-
tic – he has left Britain and now lives in Canada, and bases his
research on cases in both countries. Over the years he has been
very concerned to look for patterns in the histories of families
where children are abused and has conducted two major stat-
istical surveys, one of all the inquiries into cases between 1960

and 1978, and another of 168 child-abuse deaths between 1972 and 1983.

When we visited Greenland in Toronto he was able to show us the high-risk family checklist he had constructed on the basis of his findings. Among the features are:

– parents under the age of twenty-four
– parents who were themselves abused in childhood
– parents of low intelligence and inadequate education
– parents who are socially isolated with no immediate family or supportive friends
– parents who abuse alcohol or drugs
– mother who is pregnant or has recently given birth
– parents with a previous record of abuse or neglect of their children
– parents with poor housing or who move frequently from one place to another
– parents with several children under four
– parents where the male partner is not the biological father of all the children
– parents who are unemployed or in poor economic circum-stances

Professor Greenland has been using his checklist for several years and the more evidence he collects the more certain he is that potentially lethal families have similar characteristics. He insists that by understanding and recognizing the common risk factors it is possible to identify about 60 per cent of the children who are in danger and to act accordingly. He does acknowledge that a smaller percentage will be abused in unforeseen, un-predictable circumstances, in what some experts call 'a one-off explosion'.

Greenland was asked by the Beckford tribunal whether he recommended that where a family showed several of the high-risk factors the children should be removed. The panel were aware that the Beckford family would have scored alarmingly high on the checklist if it had been used to assess them. But Greenland said that that would be too simple, and that, although the list could be used to justify removing a child, its greatest value was to raise large warning signals over a family and to indicate where stress could be relieved. In practice this might mean taking emergency action to rehouse a family or urgently arranging day-care for children whose parents seemed to find the strain of everyday organization difficult to deal with. Greenland accepted that improvements of this kind could alleviate some problems and reduce some threats, but he was anxious to emphasize that the checklist made sense only if all the factors were looked at together in an integrated way. He compared it to an electrical circuit where an explosion would occur when all the points linked up. He repeated several times that he thought his findings should mainly be used as a touchstone against which any changes in a high-risk family should be judged, so that optimistic reports by professional workers and assertions that the family had altered in positive ways should be treated with scepticism if the original high-risk indicators were still there.

Professor Greenland's evidence was sympathetic to social services departments which are faced with an increasing burden of child-abuse cases. He considered that they were probably the most complex, difficult and stressful cases that they were ever called on to undertake. In order to develop sufficient enthusiasm and energy the social workers tend to have a very optimistic view of what can be accomplished. They tend to exaggerate progress that has been made and they may see progress where there is none. Social workers involved in high-risk child-abuse cases tend to be inured, case-hardened as it were, to the misery and the stress. Their standards may deteriorate so that they will see a child in a very miserable condition and say, 'The child looks miserable, but not as miserable as it was a month ago.' So, he argued, the checklist should be used to protect not only the threatened child but also the social worker who may, for understandable reasons, lose sight of the objective risks, fail to see recognized alarm signals, and find himself or herself faced with the ultimate tragedy of a lethal family that has actually killed a child.

But in spite of this double value to the client and to the professional, and although the Greenland checklist and similar ones from other academic institutions have been available for some time, they have not been used by social services departments in this country. The senior social worker in the Beckford case and her managers seemed, when questioned, to be ignorant of the existence of the research. It was instructive that when we drew attention to the Greenland work in a *Panorama* television programme in the autumn of 1985 we had several inquiries from local authorities, magistrates and officers of the NSPCC, who were interested in this sort of analysis and could see its value to their work, but had never come across it either in professional training or in practice. When we mentioned this to Professor Greenland he was perplexed:

> Social service agencies seem unable or unwilling to use the research data, and it's very unnerving to spend many years as I have in this field and to find very little interest in the results and very little use made of the tools that have come out of research, which would help social services to deliver a much more efficient, caring service for our children. It's pretty depressing to see that despite all the evidence we have, despite all the recommendations of numerous inquiries into child-abuse deaths, very little has changed.

Dr Leonard Taitz, consultant paediatrician at Sheffield Children's Hospital, has suffered the same type of frustration when he has attempted to introduce objective medical criteria into the management of child-abuse cases. He believes that it is precisely because these criteria are medical that they are ignored by social services departments who consider them outside their professional universe. Dr Taitz's strongly held view, which he expressed in his expert evidence to the Beckford inquiry, is that once a family has been identified as high-risk the children should be constantly and carefully monitored, both physically and psychologically, so that growth and development are constantly under review. The child who is being abused will be retarded in every kind of way: will gain weight slowly, will be small in height, will be behind in speech, and will have learning difficulties with any new skill. If this is understood, and at-risk children are regularly examined to test their rate of progress, then that information should determine how they are treated and should override the general, subjective impressions of social workers or anyone else.

In the Beckford case there was clear evidence that Jasmine put on a considerable amount of weight, and developed very rapidly, when she spent some months with foster-parents. But that progress was ignored when the social workers decided to send her back to her lethal family. Dr Taitz told the inquiry that the medical information was sufficient reason to keep Jasmine in foster care, as she clearly thrived much better there than in her own home, and that 'failure to thrive' was a clear indication of abuse. Once Jasmine had been returned home, no one carried out any further developmental checks until she died two years later. She was not even weighed, and the post-mortem revealed that when she was killed she weighed two pounds less than she had done when she went home. For a supposedly growing child of four this by itself revealed what Dr Taitz called 'catastrophic events requiring immediate intervention'. Some time after the Beckford inquiry we asked David Bishop, the social services manager in Brent whether, on reflection, he thought that, if the medical checks had been carried out and given priority, Jasmine would not have died. After a long pause he confessed that he thought she would still be alive.

At the Sheffield Children's Hospital Dr Taitz's regular development clinics demonstrate the value of continuing medical assessment in treating children who have been abused. Here we met two sisters, Katherine and Jackie Morrell, who had been removed from their parents nearly seven years before after terrible beatings, and still came to the hospital for six-monthly checks. Katherine is now ten and Jackie seven and a half, and they live very happily with their adoptive parents and another little sister, in middle-class comfort on the outskirts of Sheffield. Both are sturdy, blonde girls, who chat cheerfully and seem quite confident about the world. But Katherine is very slow at school and attends a child-guidance clinic because she often has tantrums and nightmares and seems emotionally disturbed. It is only in the last year or two that she has caught up with the average weight and height for her age group. Dr Taitz attributes this general backwardness to her early traumas. Katherine's real mother, Laura, was only seventeen when Katherine was born, and she had two more children before she was twenty – Jackie and a younger brother, Ian.

Laura would probably be classified as 'educationally sub-normal' by a psychologist, and the doctors accept that some of her daughter's retardation may be inherited. Laura was married when she had the children, but seems to have had no support from her husband, who was also a teenager and often away.

The young couple had very little money and lived in a succession of gloomy flats and bedsitters, several times being evicted because they had failed to pay the rent. Laura was far from her own family in Durham, so there were no grannies or sisters for her to turn to for help with two demanding toddlers and a baby, and Laura was not the sort of person who found it easy to make friends. Using Professor Greenland's checklist it seems to have been a classic example of a high-risk family, and in this classic example the cumulative stresses did produce catastrophe.

Katherine was three when her mother took her to the local hospital with a fractured right arm. She was covered with bruises and was underweight, and the hospital suspected that this was a non-accidental injury. Laura strenuously denied this and Katherine eventually went home with no formal outside supervision, although the hospital did suggest to the family GP that the health visitor should keep a very careful watch on the children and that it might be sensible to get the social services involved. The health visitor saw Katherine and her sister Jackie but, as far as the records show, never weighed or measured them. Laura would not allow her to check the baby Ian, who was always said to be sleeping when she called. After several abortive visits the health visitor became concerned about the 'invisible' baby and, as she had no powers to insist on seeing him, asked local social workers to intervene. A case conference was called but no hospital doctor was included to give the disturbing information about Katherine. Before the social workers had decided what to do about the case, the baby Ian was brought to the hospital, dead. The infant was severely underweight, badly bruised, and burned by cigarettes.

Katherine and Jackie were taken into care, sent to foster-parents and later adopted. Both of them were undernourished and miserably small. They were referred to Dr Taitz's department at Sheffield Children's Hospital, and have been under his care ever since. Both little girls seemed to adjust quite easily to their new home, but when measured on the objective medical criteria Jackie seemed to be doing much better than her older sister. Jackie quickly gained weight until she was well up to her age average, learned to speak easily and has never shown any abnormal emotional or learning difficulties. Katherine's progress has been much slower, both physically and mentally. Dr Taitz is convinced that this is because the children were at different ages when they were abused and when they were fostered. Medical research suggests that very young children are less permanently affected by abuse than those between two and four. This crucial information has great significance for social-work policy.

Dr Taitz explained the scientific background when we talked to him about Katherine and Jackie. 'You will find that if you look at the development of very young children, up to about eighteen months old, you don't usually see, even in the most abusive, depriving family, sufficient evidence to suggest that the family circumstances are producing delay in development. Eighteen months is the point at which the more simple psycho-motor developmental milestones are replaced by more subtle ones – the development of speech, the development of cognitive skills – and this is where you see abused children begin to lag behind. Jackie was just under eighteen months when she went to the foster-home, and her development does not seem to have been permanently retarded.

'From about eighteen months to four years there is the most dramatic change in the infant. You go from an infant who, in developmental skills, is not much different to a chimpanzee baby, to the four-year-old who has practically all the human cognitive skills inside him. There is good evidence that children who are deprived or abused in this period are going to have severe learning difficulties later. It's not surprising, because it's been demonstrated that children like this have hormonal abnormalities. Their growth hormone, which is a neuro-hormone, is lower than it should be and there is another, which again derives from the brain, which is also very low. Cerebral abnormalities are therefore associated with the failure to thrive through this hormone imbalance. If this goes on during the two and a half years between eighteen months and four, if normal growth is missed during this very short time, the consequences are often permanent. So Katherine, who was three and a half before she was rescued, has suffered much more long-term damage than the younger sister. The significance of abuse during this age of accelerated development is part of the medical model that really does need to be understood.'

Dr Taitz's conclusion about the practical application of the 'medical model' is that children who are identified as being high-risk, and whose development measurements show a failure to thrive, should be taken into long-term care as soon as possible. He is careful to emphasize that this category of extreme cases is only a small one, but that this would have been the appropriate action with Jasmine Beckford and with Katherine Morrell, who were both clearly failing to thrive in their lethal families. Taitz does not dismiss the value of family therapy and attempts to improve parenting skills so that a natural family can be kept together, but he insists that to be effective this type of work will take many years and that a child who is in the crucial develop-ment range, between eighteen months and four years, will con-tinue to be vulnerable to permanent damage at home while the long-term rehabilitation goes on. It is wrong to expose a child to that known danger in order to try and achieve much less certain results with the whole family.

Much of this is directly contrary to social-work practice, which, for the reasons described by Professor Greenland, is based on optimistic assumptions about the capacity to change people and on a fierce belief that the bonds between natural parents and children should be preserved at almost any cost. But Dr Taitz responds by arguing that the concept of early bonding in humans (as opposed to monkeys) has been exag-gerated and that, almost by definition, a child who has been abused has not been properly bonded by its parents: 'It may be a bond of barbed wire rather than a bond of love.' Dr Taitz's view is supported by much of the recent work on fostering and adoption, notably by the paediatrician Barbara Tizard, which shows that bonds can be established with adoptive parents up to a late age. It is to be hoped that this research is given much more prominence in social-work departments in the future. Some of Dr Taitz's most disturbing evidence to the Beckford tribunal suggested that the medical and scientific information was ignored by social workers not so much because they rejected it intellectually but because they were just ignorant of its detail and significance, and considered data on a child's physical and psychological state to be either too complex or too remote from their own professional concerns to be included in their assessments and management.

When one visits the Sheffield Children's Hospital assessment centre it is easy to see how its work might intimidate the untrained outsider. A whole range of highly skilled people are employed to operate the various developmental tests on the young patients. The hospital uses the sophisticated Griffiths Test to monitor each child's psychomotor function, in a way that can provide an objective figure for this part of development, so that changes over a period of time can be easily seen. This type of testing can be learned at a very few centres in Britain, and the training is open only to qualified doctors. In Sheffield the child's emotional state is considered by a clinical psychologist who has acquired special skills in paediatric care. Not every health authority employs this type of clinical psychologist and funds to recruit more are very scarce.

Dr Taitz realizes that his system is a privileged one which he has been able to build up over many years of special effort, putting together a team who now have an international reputation in this field. He does not suggest that these functions can be readily transferred to local social-work departments. Indeed, he insists that these tests can be carried out only by people with particular medical training, but he wants social workers to be aware that this expert knowledge is available and is fundamentally important to their decisions about at-risk children.

There are, of course, other more basic tests on weight and height which are equally significant and which can be done by anyone. As the Beckford inquiry report said, 'The simplest test in the world is to put the child on a pair of scales.' But, again, weighing and measuring is not considered part of a social worker's job. Officially it is the task of a health visitor or GP. The alarming fact emerged at the Beckford inquiry, and has been confirmed by our subsequent interviews, that few people with responsibility for children in care, or under supervision by social-work departments, understand why those simple weights and measures are so critical in making objective assessments about the well-being of these children. It follows that, as in Jasmine's case, they are unconcerned when even the basic facts on growth are unavailable and regard them as irrelevant when they are presented. The senior social worker in the Beckford case was unequivocal in her statement that she did not think it significant that Jasmine had put on weight when with her foster-parents, that no one working with her had noticed any change in her development. The health visitor, who failed to weigh Jasmine for two years after she returned home, told the inquiry that she accepted the mother's reports that the child was well.

The tool which makes it possible to plot, objectively, a child's physical progress is the so-called 'percentile chart' which has been available since the 1950s. The charts are routinely issued to community health centres and are standard equipment for health visitors. Instructions about their use and interpretation are printed on the back of the charts, but they still seem to be a mystery to many health visitors and their importance has not been understood by social workers.

Percentile charts have been created by establishing various patterns of normal growth from the measurements of a very large number of children. The children's weights, heights and head circumferences have been recorded at regular intervals and different trajectories of growth have been drawn up to achieve different averages for different ages. Once the averages have been established and drawn up on the percentile chart it is quite easy to see how any particular child deviates from the average by plotting his own statistics on the chart. On the weight chart, for example, the average statistics are drawn up so that there is a middle line on the chart known as the fiftieth centile, where 50 per cent of children are heavier and 50 per cent are lighter. The two most important lines are the tenth and ninetieth centiles; the lower one means that 90 per cent of children are heavier and 10 per cent are lighter; for the higher, the reverse is the case. The chart also shows the extremes of the third and ninety-seventh centiles, and any child who falls outside these extremes should automatically be regarded as unhealthy by those caring for him. Any one child's own growth trajectory is established from his birth weight and the first four months of growth. If the child's weight falls away from the established centile, and there is no evidence of illness, then the 'failure to thrive' is a very clear alarm signal that the child is being deprived and, in a high-risk family, may be being abused.

Katherine's chart showed clearly how she had slowly climbed back to her natural centile, after falling away when she was abused as a toddler. Jasmine's incomplete record revealed the tragic history of a baby who started off very close to the fiftieth centile, and then progressively fell away until at twenty-one months (when she was in hospital for the first time with serious injuries) her weight was below the third centile. This was followed by the dramatic improvement in weight while she was in foster care, which brought her back up nearly to the twenty-fifth centile; then there was the fatal gap until the disastrous post-mortem figure showing her well below the third centile again. If the percentile chart had been used and its significance understood, Jasmine's life could have been saved. The social services manager responsible for her told us lamely, 'I think we've all learned a lot listening to what went on in the inquiry in relation to percentile charts and height and weight and developmental checks and so on.' We can only hope that his colleagues in similar positions will all have learned and taken heed of the terrible example.

The front-line responsibility for the health care of children, particularly those under five, lies, of course, with the health authorities, not with social services departments and, over the years, many of the inquiry reports on child abuse, which were included in the DHSS 1982 summary, noted that deaths often occurred when there was unsatisfactory communication between the health workers and the social workers. This pattern was certainly repeated in the Jasmine Beckford case and the first general recommendation that the inquiring panel made was: 'The duty on a local authority to co-operate with a health authority should be made more specific, to include the duty to consult.' The recommendation presupposes that the professionals will understand and act on medical information which is made available through formal consultation, and that the crucial information will itself be available.

It seems extraordinary that more than a decade before Jasmine Beckford died the report on the death of Maria Colwell (perhaps the most notorious of all child-abuse cases) drew attention to the essential part which medical assessment could play in monitoring at-risk children. 'We think', declared the report, 'that not only might such provisions have averted Maria's tragedy but that their value in similar cases is clear.' This statement appears not only in the original Colwell report but in the DHSS abstract which in its own conclusion said, 'A major characteristic of many cases is the failure to bring together all available information and to use it in a structured, objective way, by carrying out full psycho-social assessments. These require constant re-examination and revision.'

Yet four years later the social workers at the Beckford inquiry professed ignorance of this vital message. The Beckford report noted, in an exasperated tone, that 'The failure of those responsible for Jasmine to stop and ask themselves the question any normal parent would ask, namely, "Is this child passing the milestones of babyhood and childhood?" is hard to explain.' The report recommended that 'whenever social workers are engaged in child-abuse cases ... they must consult any relevant literature on the subject'. It remains to be seen whether they will. So far the recommendation, which echoes those of the past, does not seem to be trickling down to individual social services offices very fast. After the Beckford report the Social Services Inspectorate of the DHSS carried out a survey of nine local authorities and their findings were published in March 1986. This report observed, 'The importance of systematic monitoring of a child's health, growth and development was often not recognized.' It added:

> Many supervisors failed to recognize that when professionals work closely with an abusing family they may be lulled into a false sense of security and begin to identify with the parents in a way that denies the potential danger to the child. They therefore underestimate the importance of regular scheduled supervision for social workers handling those cases in order to help them maintain objectivity and to keep the primary focus on the child.

It is almost as if each and every social services department will have to experience some appalling disaster at first hand before all social workers will be prepared to accept the repeated evidence and the repeated exhortations on exactly the same subjects. It is tragic that a profession of caring literate people should appear to be obdurately resistant to information whose theme has been consistent for many years.

At the moment there is no formal part of social-work training that includes the detailed study of child development, and Dr

Leonard Taitz has described that as 'a catastrophic omission'. But in broad social-work courses designed to cover the whole spectrum of generic social work, usually in only two years, it is hard to see how more specialist medical skills could be included. Child abuse is usually taught in three or four sessions and the emphasis is on the problems of establishing and maintaining trusting personal relations with the client families. Courses which we have visited made great use of role-playing to help the students empathize with the different feelings of different members of a family under stress. Although this can give valuable insights into the ways of dealing with some practical situations, it does little or nothing to help them understand that there are objective tools for assessing these families which could at the very least enhance their own personal impressions.

The Beckford report called for a reorganization of all social-work courses so that no one could qualify without three years' training. More significantly, it suggested that there should be more specialization both in the education of social workers and in the professional practice. This underlines the trend away from the idea of general social work that we discussed in chapter 1. With any luck the cumulative experience of individual social services departments caught in a storm of national criticism following child-abuse scandals handled by inadequately informed and trained social workers (the key worker responsible for Jasmine had only three hours' instruction on abuse) may prompt the adoption of a system similar to the old Children's Officers. The DHSS study of inquiry reports shows, and the Beckford report underlines, that during the period when the specialized Children's Departments were in operation, between 1948 and 1971, there was only one major inquiry into a child-abuse case where the child was either in care or being supervised by the local authority; but since then there have been more than twenty such inquiries, each one involving a traumatic upheaval in the social services department concerned.

On the question of specific medical training for social workers, even for those who under a reformed system might specialize in child care, the expert opinion is cautious. Most paediatricians we have talked to think it would be very useful for students, or those doing in-service courses, to spend some months in children's hospital units and to observe the medical criteria by which doctors assess their young patients' well-being, but there can be no question of giving social workers a 'shadow' medical education. The doctors insist that only they can carry out the sophisticated analyses and tests that are available, for example, at the Sheffield Children's Hospital. On the other hand, all those involved in child care, and this should include teachers, play-group leaders and home helps, as well as social workers, should learn the essential facts about growth and development and be aware of the importance of medical data. This may suggest that attitudes need to change as much as levels of knowledge and that, once again, co-operation between professionals is the key to successful child-abuse work.

Obviously the professional health-care workers have the basic responsibility for protecting the health and development of any child, but, beyond that, responsibility is the ultimate role of the parent. Where the legal parents are the officers of a social services department, they are the ones who must take the initiative in seeking and acting on medical advice.

Dr Leonard Taitz, for example, does not expect to work with social workers who have the same skills as his expert teams, but he does want them to know which medical questions to ask, and to understand and give priority to the answers. Taitz, and other paediatricians specializing in this field, think that the greatest advantage of a management system which gave social workers more specialized expertise would be the increase it would provide in their practical experience of child abuse. At the moment generic workers responsible for the whole range of problems in every age group may come across very few instances of abuse in their case-load. This lack of wide experience is as disastrous as lack of information.

Taitz is aware that he himself has only gradually acquired the depth and range of understanding necessary to succeed in this highly complicated field: 'I have dealt with nearly 300 cases over sixteen years, and it is only in the last four or five years that I have begun to realize that I have some sort of consistent grip of the problem. What must it be like for a relatively inexperienced social worker who is just thrown into the firing line? You can go on all the child-abuse courses in the world, but if you do not deal with a reasonable number of cases you just do not get the feel for this very special, highly dangerous problem. If any

person has only one case on at a time, over a five-year period
they might have four cases altogether, and that simply is not
going to enable them to get the adequate experience to make
sensible decisions.'

So although knowledge of the high-risk checklists and the
medical data can act as the bottom-line protection for social
workers who want to avoid disastrous mistakes, the more subtle
application of these objective standards can be developed only
through experience.

Dr Taitz demonstrated this very graphically with one particular case which we saw him handling in Sheffield. Paul, aged
nine months, a large, strong baby of the type that is sometimes
unkindly called 'a bruiser', had been admitted to the hospital
with bad bumps and grazes which his mother Rhoda said had
been caused by falling down stairs. She was a pale seventeen-
year-old, so frail-looking that it was hard to imagine her giving
birth to bouncing Paul, who spent a great deal of time shouting,
both cheerfully and angrily, and trying to pull himself to his feet
with the aid of the bars on his hospital crib. Rhoda was living
with her boyfriend, who was not Paul's father but who, according to the doctors and nurses, seemed to take a kindly interest
in the baby when he came to the hospital. Rhoda lived in her
own council flat, which she had been allocated because she was
a single mother, and financially she relied on her various state
benefits.

When we met her Rhoda looked exhausted, and spoke feelingly about broken nights and the problems of handling an
infant who was growing as energetically and noisily as Paul. She
said frankly that she welcomed the break while he was in
hospital. It was easy to understand, as we talked to her, how
she had at first enjoyed her new-born baby and the status he
had brought her, and how she had then grown alarmed by her
responsibility and was now afraid of what the future with an
active toddler might be.

The critical question was: had she or her boyfriend assaulted
Paul, or were his injuries genuinely accidental? We, the visitors,
were inclined to think that Rhoda had battered him. True, Paul
was putting on weight and showed no signs of being retarded,
but as Dr Taitz had explained, such evidence of abuse would
probably not show up in such a young child. But Taitz, the

experienced expert, decided to give Rhoda the benefit of the doubt and send Paul back home, although at the same time he gave strict instructions to the local health visitor and GP, and set up a regular system of appointments for Rhoda to bring the baby back to his clinic to be monitored. He argued that Rhoda had help from her mother and an elder sister who both lived nearby and were regularly in touch, and her sister had supported the story about accidental injuries. Taitz thought the whole family had been alarmed and shocked by what had happened to Paul. The boy's aunt, herself the mother of two young children, had been to the hospital and had shown great concern.

Taitz had looked for what he calls 'harbinger injuries' on Paul, ones like bruises behind the ear or cigarette burns (which are rarely accidental), but had found none. He concluded that although it was quite possible that Rhoda had hit the baby, at the end of her tether in a fit of tired rage, such an incident would probably be a one-off explosion and, if she was given sufficient help, she would probably manage in the future. He felt it was a knife-edge case and that there would be real dangers if she became pregnant again quickly, took up with a new boyfriend who was hostile to Paul, or moved away from her own family and found herself isolated, without friendly support.

Dr Taitz's sensitive instincts, combined with his vast knowledge of the practical ways in which parents and families react to stress, gave him the confidence to go against some of the objective factors that might have led an informed, but less experienced, person to take an exaggeratedly defensive position and bring Paul into care immediately. This, of course, is the danger of a rigid application of any set of rules or criteria which completely override subjective judgement. It has recently been suggested that, in the wake of the immensely damaging criticism of social-work practice in the Beckford report, social workers may now react by automatically removing all abused children from their families. This, of course, has been the basis of the outcry about the large numbers of children taken into care on Tyneside in the cases involving alleged child abuse in Cleveland. Although those with an authoritative view insist that long-term removal of children should only happen in extreme cases, they do recognize that the kind of short-term assessment under a 'place of safety' order which was being used by the Cleveland officials can be useful. Taitz told us, 'I think the natural family is the best place for the great majority of abused children, but it is important to recognize that there is an extreme end of the spectrum where it is not appropriate for a child to return to its natural parents. It is really in the ability to recognize that extreme end that the whole subtle management of child abuse lies. The whole business is about risk-taking, but it is the risk to the child, not the risk to the parents or the risk to the professional workers, that must be accurately judged and acted on.'

When the management of social workers allows adequately trained and adequately experienced professionals to handle the complex and perilous problem of child abuse, then we, the general public, can be more certain that the risky decisions are being taken authoritatively and correctly.

# 4  NEGLECT

Neglect is creeping cruelty. Today it is thought of as the most insidious form of abuse. Difficult to identify, with none of the apparent trauma of physical or sexual assault, neglect nevertheless seems to inflict just as much long-term damage as more obvious kinds of abuse. The NSPCC believes that neglect is more common than physical abuse, but even the society's expert researchers are unwilling to produce exact statistics. They know that neglect can kill, but even here it is often hard to isolate those deaths which can be exclusively attributed to neglect. The Registrar-General talks of deaths due to 'hunger, thirst, exposure and neglect' and about 200 children have fallen into this category in the last decade. But, as the NSPCC points out, this figure does not include those killed by injuries which might have been prevented if the child had not been generally neglected, or those cases where children die in fires, or other accidents at home, because they have been left alone. 'Neglect' is such a wide concept, which involves setting standards and making judgements about how children should be cared for, that most people have been chary of exact definitions, and so of labelling individual cases except where hindsight may determine that a child was 'neglected to death'.

Historically the type of deprivation broadly described as neglect has been recognized for a very long time. A hundred years ago NSPCC workers reported on thousands of children who were described as 'skin and bone children, children in close sour-smelling rooms, in filthy insufficient rags, on rotten beds and in untended sickness'. Fifty years ago the Children and

Young Persons Act of 1933 produced a legal definition of neglect:

> A parent or other person legally liable to maintain a child or
> young person shall be deemed to have neglected him in a
> manner likely to cause injury to his health if he has failed to
> provide adequate food clothing or lodging for him or if,
> having been unable to provide such food clothing medical
> aid or lodging, he has failed to take steps to procure it to
> be provided.

In other words poverty, or any social stress, is not a sufficient
excuse to release parents from the obligation to provide the
minimum material comforts needed to prevent a child from
suffering physical hardship.

Neglect may be as culpable as beating or rape. The most
recent official pronouncements on neglect acknowledge that
children can suffer from emotional as well as practical neglect,
that lack of love and attention may stunt a child's happy development and growth in ways that are as important as lack of food
and warmth. 'Government Guidelines on Child Abuse', issued
by the DHSS to local authorities in 1986, defined emotional
ill-treatment as the 'severe adverse effect on behaviour and
emotional development caused . . . by persistent or severe neglect
or rejection'. But the critics have been quick to point out that
there is no definition of 'persistent' or 'severe'.

Those who have considered the problem from a practical as
well as a theoretical standpoint most often quote the definition
given by an American expert, N. A. Polansky, who in 1976
compiled a 'Profile of Neglect for the United States Department
of Health Education and Welfare'. He said that neglect occurred
when 'a caretaker responsible for a child either deliberately or
by extraordinary inattentiveness permits the child to experience
avoidable present suffering or fails to provide one or more
of the ingredients generally deemed essential for developing a
person's physical, intellectual and emotional capacities'.

Although this is a clear-cut statement which covers all the
elements of neglect, and establishes that caretakers have a
responsibility for avoiding it, the American definition still begs
some of the important questions that bother today's social
workers and others who have the job of intervening in families
where child neglect is suspected. As we have seen, social workers

and even health officials are often ignorant of the objective
medical standards by which a child's development can be
charted, and are also reluctant to intrude what they feel may be
alien English middle-class assumptions about child-rearing and
patterns of family life into homes which may provide perfectly
good care based on different cultural foundations. This has
become a more acute problem as Britain has been transformed
into a multi-racial society, where the welfare agencies feel they
have no right to impose their own ideas about what ingredients
they may deem 'essential for developing a person's physical,
intellectual and emotional capacities'. At a less sophisticated
level, social workers have always been chary about making
sweeping judgements that a child who appears grubby or ill-
kempt, or who is always playing in the streets, is being neglected
in any serious way. Even when it is discovered that children
have been frequently left alone without any supervision, this
can often be explained as practical disorganization rather than
deep-seated neglect.

In this area, as in so many others, the authorities ultimately
responsible for protecting children from abuse acknowledge that
they have no systematic comprehension of neglect and how to
deal with it. David Larter, Chief Social Services Officer of the
London Borough of Redbridge, told a recent national conference
in Britain on this subject:

> What we do not know with any confidence is how severe
> does neglect have to be before it is unacceptable, and to
> whom, and at what point is intervention justified. There is
> a lack of clarity about definition; lack of clarity about which
> family characteristics and behaviours are significant in
> producing child neglect as its outcome; considerable
> uncertainty about judging interventions and more
> particularly about their impact.

It is precisely this genuine uncertainty which has caused enormous difficulties in the practical management of neglectful families and, in extreme cases, led to the deaths of children who
had been recognized to be at risk, but where intervention had
been tentative and inadequate.

The case of baby Malcolm Page, who died in 1979, aged thirteen months, of hypothermia, malnutrition and gangrene, is a classic story of the 'neglect of neglect' by welfare agencies involved with a problem family whose many difficulties obscured the life-threatening danger to one child.

Edwina and Peter Page had been married for four years when their fourth child, Malcolm, was born. The family lived in a council house in Tilbury, Essex, where Mr Page was employed as a stock controller taking home £56 a week, after rent and other deductions had been paid. There was never any suggestion that the Page family was particularly poor, or that bad economic circumstances affected their ability to look after themselves and their children adequately. Peter Page appeared to be a typical member of the community of solid, unskilled workers who formed the majority of the population in Tilbury. He had traditional views about family roles and played very little part in looking after the succession of babies born to the couple in the first few years of their marriage. Edwina Page was eighteen years old and seven months pregnant on her wedding day, and professional assessments described her as 'child-like', although technically she was not mentally retarded. After baby Malcolm died, psychiatrists reported that Edwina's IQ was 86, so-called 'dull normal', and her attitudes were described as 'fatalistic and resigned'. It is not clear whether the experts thought she developed these attitudes because of the circumstances of her life or whether she simply had a pessimistic, negative personality.

One important recurring pattern which does emerge from the scanty research done on neglectful families is that this type of abuse, in contrast to physical or sexual assault, is usually perpetrated by the mother rather than the father. After all, in most families it is still true that the primary responsibility for the day-to-day care of small children lies with the mother. In the majority of reported cases the mother has not neglected her children malevolently, or with a conscious attempt to harm them, but is simply incapable of looking after them. David Larter has referred to these women as 'disabled' mothers whose personal characteristics of apathy and futility may eventually lead them to give up any attempt to nurture their children and who may just leave them to die: Edwina Page falls into this category of ultimately hopeless mothers.

The official report on the Page case by Essex local authorities stated, 'There is no reason to think that Mrs Page did not love her children but because of her own deficiencies she had great difficulties in looking after them properly and caring for the house and keeping it to a reasonable standard.' The retrospective report is confident about using the words 'properly' and 'reasonable' in the context of a tragedy where baby Malcolm Page had died. But what is alarming about the history of the case is that these types of judgements were not consistently applied by any one of a series of social workers and health workers as they dealt with the family. The professional helpers were, after all, intended to help Mrs Page overcome her disabilities as a mother and prevent the children being disastrously neglected.

The Page family first came to the attention of their local social services department in November 1975, when they were about to have their gas supply cut off because they had failed to pay a large bill. At this time Peter and Edwina had two children, Samantha and Simon, and were living in a brand-new centrally heated council house which they had been allocated a year before. Over the next few months the Pages turned up on the social workers' files several times, either through other financial crises or because there was reported marital trouble exacerbated by the presence of Mr Page's father, who had moved in with his son and daughter-in-law. At one stage social workers visited because they had learned that Peter Page had left home, but Edwina seemed quite sanguine about her situation, which turned out to be very temporary. Apart from some instant advice, nothing further was done to intervene.

The next major domestic drama occurred when the family was threatened with eviction by the council's housing department because they were so far behind with the rent. Before the council could take drastic action or social services could try to work out an alternative plan of campaign, the Pages 'did a flit' and removed themselves to the neighbouring borough of Grays. The housing department described the recently pristine house which they had left as being 'in a filthy mess', and before it could be relet it had to be fumigated and scrubbed out with disinfectant.

A pattern of disorganization and stress was already visible but, perhaps because each incident seemed isolated at the time, and because Peter and Edwina Page constantly professed their ability to cope with their own problems, every encounter with the social services was treated on an *ad hoc* basis. No systematic assessment was made of the family as a whole and, in particular, the needs and condition of the children were ignored. The later report on Malcolm's death noted that a 'social history' report should have been written of the family at this early stage which might then have spotted some of the potential areas of danger and provided a basic analysis to be used in managing subsequent problems.

Fairly soon the Page family were rehoused on another Tilbury council estate, but this time they were allotted a much older terraced house with open fires and a back boiler to heat the water. The kitchen and bathroom were old-fashioned and the house, in Tillett Place, was in a corner of a rather rundown area which had a reputation for accommodating a high proportion of people with previous records of debt or destructiveness. For Mrs Page, who had been unable to maintain her previous home with all its 'mod cons', No. 3 Tillett Place was to prove a completely overwhelming challenge. Her third baby, Suzanne, was born in January 1977, followed eleven months later by Malcolm. Twenty-two-year-old Edwina Page was now responsible for four children under the age of five.

Malcolm was born on 27 December 1977 and, shortly after Mrs Page left hospital with her new baby, the local health visitor tried to make a routine call to see if all was well. Mrs Page had been anaemic after the birth and the health visitor was concerned because she had not followed up on her treatment when she went home. But no one appeared to be at home when the health visitor called and she made six more unsuccessful attempts to get into the house. Finally, on 7 March 1978 Mrs Page replied to her knock on the door and, somewhat reluctantly, allowed her inside to see the baby and the other children. The health visitor was horrified by what she found. Her report described the state of the house and the children in vivid detail:

> The living room was squalid and there was a foul smell. The carpet was so thick with grime that it was black and very sticky; the settee was grubby and the walls were covered in dirty paper, some of which was peeling. Samantha, the eldest child, was in the room and naked but not dirty although her hair was matted and her face was grubby. Simon was half-

dressed and asleep on the settee; he had a nappy rash on his bottom, mucus on his face and was grubby. Suzanne (just over a year old at this time) was sitting in a pram; her hair was matted with cradle cap and there was dried brown mucus all over her face and ears. She was wearing plastic pants over a disposable nappy and the pants were hanging and saturated with urine. The glands in her neck were swollen and she was exceptionally pale. The fontanelle had not closed as it should have done which suggested she had been receiving the wrong type of food. The pram she was in was smothered in a dark-brown sticky substance and was absolutely filthy, and she was picking broken biscuits out of it to eat. The new baby was asleep in another pram tightly wrapped in cot bedding.

When Malcolm woke, Mrs Page refused to allow the health visitor to undress and examine him but she could see that he too had cradle cap, was chesty and had a nasal discharge. She described him as 'a floppy baby with poor muscle tone'.

Mrs Page seemed unable to give any coherent explanation for these terrible conditions and became very angry when the health visitor suggested that she needed a home help. On 13 March the health visitor returned, this time with a social worker who had been alerted by her report. Mrs Page again refused to open the door but, with the help of a neighbour, they managed to persuade her to agree to another appointment a few days later. When the social worker kept the prearranged appointment on 16 March she found the house and the children still in a very dirty, unkempt state. Mrs Page appeared to have made no effort to improve things, although she had had advance warning of the visit and it was by now over nine days since the health visitor had first been inside No. 3 Tillett Place. The social worker described Mrs Page as being nervous and depressed, and she too suggested that the whole family would benefit if the social services department provided them with a home help. Mrs Page again rejected the idea.

Over the next few weeks the social services agencies paid a great deal of attention to the Page family. There were several visits by the health visitor, by different social workers, including a senior member of the team, and by the senior home-help organizer for the district. All of them were appalled by what they found and tried to impress on both Mrs Page and her husband, who was present during some of the visits, that unless they took immediate steps to clean up the living conditions the children might be placed in care. Every time this possibility was mentioned Mrs Page became extremely upset and distressed and it was apparent to all the professional workers that she desperately wanted to keep the children at home. She had in no way rejected them emotionally, even though she seemed incapable of caring for them.

Mrs Page's distress at the threat of losing the children was translated into limited practical action, and she did do some basic housework in the living room and the kitchen. But on 30 March the children were still in 'a sorry state' and, on this occasion, the social worker, Susan Riches, succeeded in inspecting the bedrooms, which the Pages had refused to allow before, and found that all three smelt, that there were dried faeces ground into the floors and that the bedding was soaked with urine. Edwina and Peter Page were told that a home help was to be assigned to the family and that she would come every weekday and work for several hours whether they welcomed this assistance or not. But this well-intentioned attempt to take a directional grip on the chaos in the Page household was frustrated because when the home help reported for work she nearly always found either that there was no sign of Mrs Page and the children or that there was a note pinned to the front door saying that the family had gone out.

By the third week of April the situation had reached another crisis; Mrs Page had failed to take the children for medical check-ups, although the clinic was very near and both the social worker and the home help had offered to accompany her. She was still only allowing the helper to come into the house intermittently, and refusing to let anyone outside the family go upstairs.

On 27 April the social services department held a full case conference on the Page family and, as a result, it was decided to take out Place of Safety Orders on the children, which would enable them to be fostered, at least temporarily. When Susan Riches went to Tillett Place to explain the decision there was a predictable storm, but eventually the children were taken away

and placed with two separate sets of foster-parents. As a result
of this extreme action Mr and Mrs Page seemed to be shocked
into co-operation, and appeared to understand the advice that
the children might be allowed to return if there was a substantial
improvement in their home living conditions. Over the next
month both parents made noticeable efforts to clean and even
to redecorate parts of the house. The upstairs rooms were
inspected and reported to be much more hygienic, although
there were still very few bedclothes for the children.

At the end of May the juvenile court ruled that all the children
should be the subject of care orders which, of course, gave the
local authority legal parental rights over them. But the social
services representative said at the hearing that it was not the
intention of the department to prolong the children's absence
from home and, on 16 June, the two older children went back,
followed a few days later by Suzanne and Malcolm. The social
worker noted that all the family seemed pleased to be together
again and that the living room was clean and tidy.


The later official inquiry into Malcolm's death criticized the
superficiality of the analysis which led first to the decision to
foster the children and then to the subsequent decision to send
them home. Both decisions seemed to have been based solely on
the physical state of the house, at the beginning and end of the
fostering period respectively. There was no attempt to assess
the children's state of development on any of the objective
medical criteria available; no attempt to consider Mrs Page's
mental state or Mr Page's role in the family. The inquiry report
stated that 'the picture presented showed poor maternal health,
gross neglect of the children, debt and disorder – a family
overwhelmed and out of control with a mother who was apa-
thetic and lacking in motivation and initiative to change, and a
father failing to take responsibility or support his wife'. None
of these deep problems was reflected in the optimistic assumptions of the social worker that the family could make a fresh
start because the parents had made the home habitable and Mr
Page was earning enough to provide them with their material
needs. There seems to have been no professional acknow-
ledgement that the pattern of severe neglect might be chronic

and stem from much deeper roots than inadequate household management.

Very recently the NSPCC Research Unit, led by Susan Creighton, has assembled the available evidence on dangerously, persistently neglectful families, and has drawn up a model of the circumstances in which parents are most likely to abuse their children in this way. The most crucial findings seem to relate to the character and emotional state of the mother. An emotionally immature mother, particularly one who is unsupported by her children's father, is often unable to comprehend the level and continuity of responsibility involved in caring adequately for young children – hence David Larter's reference to a 'disabled' mother. The tendency to neglect is exacerbated when a mother is young in years as well as maturity and when she has several children in quick succession.

Other indicators which the researchers point to are: an unclean house with ingrained dirt and smell, poor personal hygiene, unstable marital relations, bad housekeeping and erratic money management leading to debt and financial crises which, in turn, often lead to the family moving often from home to home. The findings show that more than a third of families who have been identified as seriously neglectful have been in their present accommodation for less than a year, and the general picture is of disorganization and failure to cope with the practicalities of everyday life, coupled with a more deep-seated psychological sense of inadequacy. The NSPCC summarize their findings by saying 'there is a general low standard of parenting combined with multiple stress factors which make crises difficult to cope with'.

In retrospect it is easy to say that had this model been available to the field workers involved with the Page family they might have felt justified in recommending that the children be fostered on a long-term basis. But the basic rules of contemporary social work which insist that the family must be judged as a unit apply as forcibly to neglect cases as to cases of physical or sexual abuse. 'The family seems to have improved and must, therefore, be given the benefit of the doubt; to act otherwise would undermine the element of trust on which successful relations with professional workers should be based.' This is the underlying philosophy which has proved the basis for many decisions in child-abuse cases, where the special needs of the children are not given priority. The Page case was no different. Mr and Mrs Page followed the advice they were given after the children were fostered – though a cynic might note that they did so only under duress – and therefore the social services, lulled by their own rule of optimism, reunited the family. Once again the principle of family unity and rehabilitation was paramount in directing the fate of the children.

Within six weeks of the Page children's return to the family home, the social worker was already getting reports that the new-found standards of cleanliness were slipping. Although the home help was visiting regularly, Mrs Page would not allow her to work in the bedrooms, which were again described as smelly with wet and stained linen; on one occasion the social worker found dirty nappies piled up in the living room. The home help said there was little food in the kitchen. Mrs Page failed to keep appointments at the health clinic for the children to be weighed and checked, even though the social worker and the health visitor both came to remind her of the dates and to accompany her on the half-mile walk to the clinic. Mrs Page always produced a lame excuse for why it was impossible for her to leave the house on that particular day, and the excuses were accepted.

As the children were then in care, although living with their parents, the social worker had the statutory right to insist that medical examinations be carried out and, at a practical level, her powers gave her the responsibility to ensure that the children had adequate food and bedding. But at a case conference on 10 August Susan Riches, the social worker, was simply recommended to discuss the unsatisfactory situation with the family 'in blunt terms', and to warn them that a failure to improve could lead to the children being taken away again. It was later noted that Miss Riches had an extremely heavy workload of fifty-four cases, including ten which concerned child abuse, though neither she nor her immediate superior had any specific training in this area.

The Page family drifted along. Threats to remove the children led to hysterics from Mrs Page and a short-term blitz on the care of the house and the family. Mrs Page was induced to take the children to the health clinic where they were judged to be reasonably fit and well nourished, although suffering from impetigo and nappy rash. By the autumn, the home help and the social worker felt that on the whole the situation was improving. Although there were times when the children were wet and dirty or there was very little food in the kitchen, Mrs Page convinced the professional workers that these were just very temporary difficulties which she could handle.

As the year drew on, life at Tillett Place seemed to go downhill again. The normal stress of winter existence with young children was perilously exacerbated by Mrs Page's own lack of physical and psychological resilience. She complained of depression, of tiredness and of sore throats. Samantha, the eldest child, was away from school because she was ill, and her younger brothers and sister had colds. But the family was excited about enjoying Christmas festivities and the social worker did not feel that there were fundamental, let alone life-threatening, problems.

Nineteen-seventy-nine began and from the middle of January the home help once again found that she could not get into the house regularly. But this alarm signal did not produce any crisis action by her supervisors or the social worker. On 26 January the home help was admitted and went upstairs to find that the bedrooms were what she described as 'grubby but not filthy'; the rooms were cold with no heating at all and the bedclothes were damp. On 29 January Susan Riches visited the Pages in the evening. She did not go upstairs and was told that the two youngest children, Suzanne and Malcolm, were asleep in their bedrooms. The home help visited on 30 January, 2 February and 5 February; she did not go upstairs on any of these days and did not see one-year-old Malcolm who, she assumed, was upstairs in his cot. During these various visits Mr Page was said to feel that 'things were a lot better than they had been', Mrs Page 'seemed cheerful enough' and the older children, who were visible, were described as 'looking well'.

In the last week of January and the first week of February the air temperature in Tilbury hovered around freezing for most of the time; the weather was pronounced 'bitingly cold'. On 6 February at about 1 p.m. a call was received at Grays, Essex, ambulance station to go to No. 3 Tillett Place. The ambulance arrived in less than ten minutes and the driver collected

Malcolm, who seemed to be unconscious. He died the next day in Basildon Hospital from hypothermia and malnutrition. Hypothermia is a body state which is reached when the body temperature is well below normal, and in a child of Malcolm's age a body temperature recorded below 36° centigrade would cause concern. When Malcolm was admitted to hospital his actual body temperature was 18.5° centigrade. The post-mortem showed that there was no identifiable trace of foodstuff in his stomach contents. He had gangrene in five toes.

A professor of physiology who gave his opinion on the case said that a child who was extremely cold and hungry would lie very still in his cot and make the minimum of movement or sound. If he was left like this for any length of time he would lose consciousness and, in the expert's opinion, Malcolm had probably been unconscious for more than twenty-four hours before Mrs Page asked a neighbour for help. The neighbour, in turn, summoned an ambulance. The physiologist's opinion, which he gave to the subsequent official inquiry, was that Malcolm's death resulted from severe neglect in the provision of adequate food, clothing, warmth and cleanliness.

Mr and Mrs Page served prison sentences for the wilful neglect of Malcolm, but both have now been released, and both are clearly still young enough to produce another family of children, whether together or separately. It is not known if either of them has received the sort of help or therapy which might make it possible for them to become different, capable parents. No one connected with the case thinks this is probable, and it seems particularly unlikely that the type of long-term treatment which might have resolved Edwina Page's psychological immaturity and depression has been available to her.

Malcolm's 'legal parents', Essex County Council Social Services, were severely censured by the official inquiry which investigated the circumstances of his death. There was particular criticism of the stark contrast between the apparently unconcerned assessments of the professional workers in the weeks before Malcolm's death and the horrifying reports of the detective chief inspector who investigated the house immediately afterwards. The police evidence spoke of a dirty, cold kitchen containing a small amount of food and a lot of dirty washing.

There was a smell of urine in the hall which became stronger as the inspector went upstairs. On the landing there was excrement just lying on the floor, and the same was found in all three bedrooms. The rear bedroom, where Malcolm slept, was described in coolly factual terms.

> There was a double bed and a cot, the bed had a double mattress on it which was very heavily stained and sopping wet with urine. There was a white blanket on the bed and lying on top of this were lumps of excrement, and there was excrement ground into the blanket which was again soaked with urine. The cot in the room had a small mattress and there was no other bedding in the cot. The mattress had a plastic cover and smelt very strongly of urine. There were at least twelve empty milk bottles lying in different positions on the floor.

After Malcolm's death, his elder sister Samantha was taken to hospital suffering from burns which were thought to have been caused by lying in urine.

The inquiry panel acknowledged that none of the official visitors to Tillett Place had been in the Page children's bedrooms since 26 January, but they were unable to accept that conditions could have deteriorated from 'acceptable' to the state described by the policeman on 8 February, in just two weeks. The report emphasized that, at a minimum, the social worker, home help and health visitor were individually and collectively responsible for ensuring that the children had clean, dry, warm bedding.

During the investigation all the professional workers admitted that they had rarely ventured upstairs to look at the bedrooms and that they probably judged everything else in the house by rather low standards. The inquiry report noted that it was a common trap to 'adjust expectations downwards to the level at which a family can perform. One way of reading the statements about the condition of the house as "not too bad" is "not too bad for the Pages".' Once again the social-work ethic, the determination to be positive and to think the best of a client family, distorted the objective standards of the visiting workers who would never have accepted the so-called improved conditions of the Page household as anywhere near satisfactory for their own families. And yet the local authority was acting *in loco parentis* to the Page children and could have, and should have, imposed conditions for the children's care. Again, to quote from the inquiry into Malcolm's death, 'The care orders were obtained because the social services department considered they needed a measure of control of the family situation. The care orders should have provided a sharp focus from which to view the case, i.e. the welfare of the children and the adequacy of parental care.' Malcolm's own needs, his rights as a child to a healthy, happy existence, which might be best led separately from his natural family, were disastrously ignored both by his biological parents and by those who had the statutory responsibility and authority to care for him.

In the years since Malcolm Page died, the experts have become increasingly concerned about the rising numbers of neglect cases and about the evidence that this type of abuse is directly related to particular social circumstances and stress. The research of the NSPCC has found that single mothers are disproportionately associated with child neglect, and thus it follows with bleak logic that, in a decade when the number of single-parent families has risen by 25 per cent, child neglect will have increased. One of the forms of neglect which seems to go hand in hand with lone mothering is regularly leaving young children alone for long periods, with all the possibilities of domestic accidents that this suggests, as well as the lack of basic care that babies and toddlers must suffer if they are often left to fend for themselves.

The current case of three-year-old Sandy Philip and her mother Jan, who like the Page family live in eastern outer London, shows many of the difficulties of today's immature, unsupported mothers whose children often end up in care. Jan is now nineteen. She was sixteen when her daughter was born, the product of a passionate but passing relationship with a young man whom she had met at school. Jan had planned to train for a skilled job but, like a surprising number of girls of her age, decided to abandon this ambition and to go ahead with her pregnancy.

Several social workers, dealing with very young mothers in different parts of the country, have told us that, although few of their clients are formally religious, there is a considerable aesthetic revulsion from abortion among many of today's teen-agers, which is often combined with a rather incoherent longing for the status and maturity they think motherhood will confer. Unemployment among young people is high in certain areas and has become more and more widespread in the recent past. 'Having a baby' has often become a way of passing the time, of finding something to do which may, with luck, bring an independent home to an unmarried mother and take a dis-contented girl away from interfering parents and an empty, dull life. Much of this increasingly typical pattern applied to Jan Philip.

With the sort of coincidence of timing that many psychologists would consider non-accidental, Jan became pregnant at about the same time that her divorced mother remarried. To start with, Jan found her mother very helpful and supportive but then the complex inter-generation relationships seemed to create family trouble, first between Jan and her stepfather, and then between the two women. Jan 'went on the social' and soon after her confinement moved out of her mother's home, at a time when the flurry of attention she had received when baby Sandy was born was boosting her confidence and her enjoyment of her new role. Jan loved dressing up her pretty little baby and showing her off to friends, who were often either stuck at home without a job, or else caught in the grind of routine work.

But, as time went on, the novelty of motherhood wore off, the docile infant became a bouncing baby and then a demanding toddler, and Jan found the task of looking after her extremely demanding. She was now nearly eighteen years old, living by herself in a pleasant, small council flat, and she felt completely alone and dominated by Sandy, who was now too big to carry around all the time or take out in the evenings. Jan was still on bad terms with her own mother, who by that time had another baby of her own from her remarriage, and was certainly not going to volunteer to be a babysitter for her granddaughter. Jan's friends, who had seemed envious when they had viewed Sandy in her pram, were less enthusiastic about taking charge of a boisterous little girl, and were anyway caught up in a social round of teenage life which Jan felt desolate at missing. She was quite closely in touch the local child-care clinic and she complained about her isolation and depression to a health visitor, who recommended that Jan should 'try and expand her horizons', 'go out and make friends with other young mums', people who might sympathize with her situation and help out from time to time.

Jan followed some of the advice. She did start to go out and about, but with her single young friends who seemed much more congenial than the staid couples recommended by the health visitor who were part of a local babysitting circle. Jan began to be more and more daring about leaving Sandy on her own in the evenings. Once the little girl had gone to sleep she would prop a bottle in her cot in case she woke and was lonely or hungry. Then Jan would go off to the local pub.

Soon Jan had a new lover, Ron. He was very seductive and she spent longer and longer evenings with him, sometimes not returning until the early morning. Sandy always seemed safe in her cot when her mother came back and, in the centrally heated flat, there were none of the well-known hazards of paraffin stoves or open heaters to threaten a dangerous fire. But one Saturday evening Jan's 'luck' ran out when her neighbours, who had earlier been disturbed by the noise of persistent crying from her flat, were woken by the noisily cheerful arrival back of herself and Ron at 2.30 in the morning. The next day Jan and the neighbours 'had words', and on Monday the local NSPCC office was presented with a lurid story of Jan's immorality and irresponsibility. When an inspector later called on Jan she was genuinely shocked to learn that her behaviour constituted a formal case of 'neglect by leaving alone'. She protested that she always took steps to make sure that Sandy was safe, that she loved her daughter very much, and that her social life made her a better mum because she was not depressed as she had been before and could give Sandy better care and attention when she was at home with her.

It was true that the NSPCC inspector, and the social worker later brought into the case, could find nothing physically wrong with Sandy, who appeared to be well fed and slept in a clean cot in a warm room. The professional workers tried to impress on Jan that the child might well suffer emotionally if she constantly woke to find herself alone at night, and that the risks of harm were much more complicated than the straightforward damage which might occur if the active toddler climbed out of her cot. Jan was alarmed when she discovered that both 'leaving alone' and 'emotional neglect' were (as they had been since 1980) sufficient grounds for Sandy to be placed on the 'at-risk' register, and apparently she sincerely promised to mend her ways.

That promise was made just over a year ago. Today Sandy is on the at-risk register and Jan has been told that her daughter may soon be taken into foster care. The professionals in the case are not hopeful that even this dire threat will change Jan's attitude to the child, which seems to be a mixture of genuine affection and incurable irresponsibility. After the first reported incidents of neglect the social services tried to support Jan by arranging for the little girl to go to a day nursery three days a week and making contacts for her with local babysitters. But this type of help did not suit Ron, who was at work during the day and did not want Jan to fulfil her part of babysitting 'contracts' by spending some evenings looking after other people's children.

The social worker succeeded in convincing Jan that it was far less harmful to Sandy if Ron were to spend nights in her flat than if the child were left alone. But this still did not solve the problem because Ron and Jan wanted to go out, especially at the weekends, and it soon became clear that Ron's sway over his girlfriend was far more powerful than the strictures of the social services, or even than her feelings for Sandy. A senior social worker, familiar with the apparently hopeless triangle of Jan, Sandy and Ron, said rather poignantly, 'I'd like to be able to give Jan some maturing fertilizer so that she'd grow up quickly before we're forced to take Sandy away. She is certainly not a wicked person, and could be a good parent, but at the moment she is really a child herself.'

Jan and Sandy's story is not one of gross physical degradation or cataclysmic events but it nonetheless alarms those who see this type of neglectful abuse steadily increasing as more and more lone mothers battle with the normal stresses of bringing up their children, often made worse by their own immaturity and social isolation. And although the researchers can plot rising numbers, neglect continues to be a neglected area of abuse, perhaps simply because it presents such intractable problems. One NSPCC paper summarized the extreme difficulty of managing these cases successfully in this way:

> How the professional chooses any particular form of treatment will depend on ... whether he or she believes that parenting skills can be taught, whether relationships within the family can be changed, and what part material problems and stress factors play in causing child neglect. Finally the professional has to decide when to close the case – has there been any change? Is the change sufficient to ensure adequate parenting for this child? Neglect cases tend to stay open for a long time due to the difficulties involved in deciding what an acceptable level of child care would be.

Professional uncertainty in the face of increasing case-loads of more complex examples of neglect is particularly alarming because such long-term studies as there are suggest that this type of abuse is just as likely to recur from generation to generation as the other more obvious forms of physical and sexual assault. The neglected child who grows up with a low sense of self-esteem, and a lack of first-hand experience of practical nurturing and emotional warmth, may well become a neglectful parent. The cycle of abuse goes on and on and there seems to be no confident answer about when and how it can successfully be broken.

# 5  WITNESS FOR
## THE PROSECUTION

The 1980s have uncovered a new dimension to the problem of child abuse: sexual abuse within the family. Interest has been fanned by newspaper and magazine articles, and by a number of powerful television programmes. The NSPCC have contributed their not inconsiderable campaigning skills. They claim there was a 90 per cent increase in reported cases, between 1984 and 1985, and a 126 per cent increase between 1985 and 1986.

It might be convenient to think that this sudden explosion is another sickness which the permissive society has thrown up. But that is far from the truth. Adults have been using children for their own sexual gratification for a long time. It was possible to dismiss such practices as the work of perverted men in plastic macs who stalked their prey and lurked in dark alleyways – men who occasionally were so deranged that they killed the children they molested. It was quite a different matter to think that fathers, stepfathers, uncles, grandfathers could be habitually involved in such things.

But once attention had been focused on children's needs and it was considered appropriate to interfere to protect them against parental cruelty, parental neglect and parental deprivation, it was inevitable that other hidden and traditionally secret forms of abuse would come to light. Recently teachers, social workers and doctors have begun to recognize some of the signs, to listen to the children, and to face the fact that there is a problem. Social services departments throughout the country report that they are being 'inundated' with cases of sexual abuse for which they have no expertise.

Leeds is no exception to the general trend in Britain. At one of the largest hospitals there, they had about ten cases a year in 1983, and by 1986 they were seeing up to 200 cases. The paediatrician in that hospital, Dr Jane Wynne, who is 'seeing more cases than we can handle at the moment', has become a leading expert in the field. She checks all the children who have been physically abused now to see whether they have also been sexually abused. Until recently she had not done that. 'Things had been there but we hadn't been looking and thinking about it,' she told us. 'We started reading the literature from America and we realized figures there were suggesting that one in three had some sexual experience, one in ten within the family and one in a hundred was incest. We think these figures are right for this country. But we also found that a lot of mothers whose children were being physically abused told us they themselves had been sexually abused and we realized what devastating effects it was having on them as adults. They had difficulty making relationships and they hadn't had help themselves. So we started to think a bit more about it.' Once she and her colleagues began to look and listen more carefully, they found the numbers dramatically increased. 'The situation is quite over-whelming at the moment,' she said, 'and it's proving difficult because we feel we're being swamped by the large number that are coming to see us.'

It is not easy to gauge exactly how widespread the problem is since the definition of sexual abuse seems to vary so widely. Figures from the USA show that 38 per cent of women in San Francisco claimed they were sexually abused before the age of eighteen; a further study in New England indicated 19 per cent of all students had been sexually abused, and the largest sample in the UK estimated 'conservatively' that 10 per cent of the population had been abused some time in their youth.

All the research has found that the perpetrators are male (95%) and the overwhelming majority were already known to the child. A recent UK survey asked GPs, police surgeons, paediatricians and child psychiatrists to report on cases of sexual abuse of children under fifteen that were known to them. They found that a staggering 43 per cent of the cases involved relatives of the child and 31 per cent involved family acquaintances. The San Francisco study showed that the overwhelming majority of the perpetrators were known to the child (89 per cent) and that stepfathers were more likely to abuse their daughters sexually than natural fathers. One in six women in the sample living with a stepfather was sexually abused compared to one in forty women living with a natural father. This study also found that only a tiny fraction of the abuse was reported to the police. So police figures are likely considerably to underestimate the problem.

Sexual abuse differs from physical abuse in several ways. Physical abuse is committed by both men and women, sexual abuse is almost entirely male. Physical abuse occurs within the family; sexual abuse is committed both inside and outside the family. Physical abuse tends to be limited to lower-income families, sexual abuse takes place in every social class. But perhaps the most important difference is that police and the law have long been involved in sexual abuse, which is a criminal offence. The police were dealing with the problem well before the social workers, paediatricians and psychologists became concerned. They rarely prosecute for physical abuse unless a child is dreadfully injured or killed. Police are willing to let the medical and social-work professions deal with most of these cases.

In Britain only about fifty people a year go on trial for the offence of cruelty and neglect, and less than half of those are imprisoned. Over five times that number are prosecuted for various counts of child sexual abuse, and most of those found guilty are imprisoned. Our attitude towards sexual abuse is far more punitive than that towards physical abuse. Although reporting in Britain is not mandatory, police are invariably informed of all allegations.

Prosecutions do not always follow the allegations because sexual abuse is not easy to detect. There are no broken bones, no bruises, no obvious scars. There can be no x-ray analysis exposing a history of unexplained fractures. Dr Wynne outlined the problem to us: 'I think we have to be careful because there are some signs which are minor, and sometimes the signs are quite gross. So, for example, if a child has been forcibly raped there will be very definite and clear signs, but if a child has been fingered there might be small abrasions on their vulva, some dilation of the vaginal orifice, absent hymen. If we see signs like that and the child tells us that they have been touched, that's good enough for us because we basically believe the children, and so far we haven't had a child tell us anything that's wrong. When it comes to looking at bottoms, occasionally we see a grossly dilated anus where clearly something has gone into it to make it wider than it should be; we also see tears, we see dilated veins, we see what we call reflex relaxation. There are quite a lot of signs. When they are gross they are clear-cut; at other times they may be consistent with finger penetration but you can still see signs.'

The signs can, however, be differently interpreted and often prove to be inconclusive. So the only real evidence is the child's account, which can be vague and confused. While certain professionals may believe a child, the courts demand a precise and exact account of events. As a consequence, many cases never even reach the courts. Others fail because of the formality of English law. Our laws insist that children appear in court and give evidence against their own fathers or whoever is accused. The frightened child often seems to be a victim not only of traumatic abuse but of the legal system itself.

One case that recently went through the courts illustrates some of the legal hurdles.

Donna Stockton walked into the social services department and said she'd had enough. She and her sister had been living with their father for the past year. Her mother had left with another man and did not want to see them. Donna was sixteen and had no one else to turn to. The tale she told the social workers made them immediately take out a care order and place both sisters in a foster-home. It is a tale that has become all too familiar. The problem was clear enough to the paediatrician who examined her, to the social worker who listened to her, and to the police who took the statements over several weeks. But it is one that the courts found particularly difficult to unravel.

Donna told the social workers that her father had been 'messing around with her' from the age of eight. Although her memories going back over a long period of time were vague, she did remember certain occasions in graphic detail. One was when she was eleven and had been out horse riding. She had come back hot and sticky because she had fallen off the horse. She limped back home and her father called to her from the store cupboard. She went in to tell him what had happened and he grabbed her, kissed her on the lips and then slowly opened her trousers, pulled down her knickers and inserted his fingers in her vagina. She recalled vividly that he had not moved his fingers, just kept them there. She had struggled and rushed off to tell her mother, who had shouted at her father and told him to leave her alone.

Donna mentioned other occasions and explained that the same thing had been happening to her sister, who was four years younger. The social workers fetched her twelve-year-old sister Shelley, who told them how their father had placed her on his knee, kissed her and inserted his fingers into her. Neither of the girls claimed that the father had had intercourse with them. But that was not unusual. The social workers have become used to bizarre sexual practices recounted to them by children. They took the girls to the police.

Donna and Shelley were made as comfortable as possible in the detective sergeant's office. They were interviewed by a woman detective and the social worker sat with them. Donna became more relaxed. She is naturally an extrovert who enjoys attention. Attractive with a round expressive face, she has sudden violent changes of mood. During the interview she showed flashes of quick temper. At other times she would become sullen. The detective felt she might prove a difficult witness. But her story was quite clear.

She claimed that her father had started 'messing around' with her when she was eight. Two months after her eighth birthday she had been sitting on the sofa watching TV with her father on one side and her sister on the other. At one point her father had put his arm tightly round her, lifted up her shirt and started to fondle her breasts. There were two other occasions when he had done the same thing, once in the bedroom and once in the kitchen. She recalled the incident after her riding accident, and was able to give dates and times for all her allegations. Crucially she described an incident the year before when her father had burst into her room, wished her good morning and then taken off his trousers and jumped into bed with her. He had stretched out on top of her, fondling her breasts and touching her at the top of her legs. She had fought him off and rushed downstairs. Three months later he had come into the bathroom while she was washing her hair and had started to fondle her breasts. She had started to cry and he had glided away. The detective, who had laboriously recorded the allegations in long hand, thought there were five possible indictments for assault.

Shelley was more hesitant. She is a boyish but joyless twelve-year-old. She seldom smiles and is very shy. The police had to drag out the story she had told the social workers. But, again, it remained remarkably consistent. She had barely remembered the incident with Donna on the sofa, although Donna had claimed she was there. She was only four at the time so it is not particularly surprising. There were two other occasions she was quite clear about, when she was nine and ten. Her father had kissed her and played with her, once in the living room and once in her bedroom, both times just before she was going off to school. The clearest incident had been the year before when her father had called her into his bedroom. There he had started to fondle her and had asked her to put her hand down his trousers. He had taken out his penis, but she had only brushed it with her hand before running off. Later she had told her sister what had happened.

The girls were both examined by a paediatrician who specializes in sexual abuse. She reported that both girls had physical symptoms compatible with penetration. Donna had had intercourse with her boyfriend and denied having had it with her father. She did admit that her father had been abusing her from the age of seven, had inserted his tongue in her mouth and had put his fingers 'up me'. The paediatrician's opinion was that the girl had been sexually abused. But it was Shelley who was the shock. Not only did she have vaginal symptoms that were compatible with intercourse, which would be unusual to say the least in a twelve-year-old. But she volunteered to the gentle, efficient doctor that her father had asked her to hold his 'willy', had inserted his fingers into her vagina and had tried to have sexual intercourse with her. The police swung into action again and interviewed Shelley about the new accusations. But she would not repeat them to the police. She stood by her original statement.

The father was brought to the station and the charges were

read out against him. He put his hand against his forehead and slumped against the counter, too shocked to talk. Later that night he was questioned for two hours. He denied all the allegations, although he refused to answer some of the questions. He said that he cuddled his daughters as any affectionate father might and occasionally got into bed with them to comfort them, but he was just a normal, loving father. After he had spent some time with him, the CID detective sensed that the allegations were true. 'Put it down to a policeman's instinct,' he mused. 'It was his evasiveness, his manner. At times he would explode, then the next minute he would be calmness itself. He would describe Donna one minute as a model teenager and the next as quite out of control. He thought himself very much the strong man. He was well built and muscly. He gave the impression of being tough and gruff. But there was something devious about him.'

What finally clinched it was when the detective put it to him that the girls had made the allegations without any apparent motive. He replied: 'If society wants to misinterpret my actions then I will have to accept what happens. Look, put it all down to me. If they say I've done it I must have done it. But it's done in love without any thought of malice or any harm towards them.' The detective then asked, 'So are you saying you have done the things they allege?' The father answered, 'I'm saying that I'll say yes to what they say happened and I'll have to bear the stigma for the rest of my life. But they will probably find it harder to bear than I will.' The police were sure after that that he would plead guilty. But three months later when he was formally charged he pleaded not guilty. The case went to trial at the crown court.

The defence felt they had a fairly reasonable case. Curiously, unlike the police they had been struck by the father's gentle, almost effeminate manner. He had had two minor previous convictions but not for sexual offences. They thought that if they could get that out into the open early on in the trial, Derek, the father, would be very credible in court. They were convinced that the elder girl had wanted to go into care because she was at daggers drawn with him and had concocted the story to get her own back. They felt that Shelley, who they rightly surmised never wanted to go to court, was merely her sister's dupe.

The social workers had not discussed the matter further with the girls after their original disclosures. They do remember clearly that the girls had given a strong impression of having regular sexual experiences with their father particularly in the last year. One of the social workers recalls asking Shelley in the car on the way back from the police when the last instance of abuse had taken place and the girl had said quite casually, 'Last Thursday.' The social worker did not appear in court. She concentrated on getting the girls settled into their foster-home, organizing new school and job, calculating financial arrangements, discussing new friends. She wanted the girls to be settled as quickly as possible, to make a clean start and build new friendships.

The day of the trial dawned. Shelley had never wanted to go to court and felt beside herself with fear. Donna, although much keener to see the case through the court, was also very nervous. Just before they went into the court the police took them to one side to explain what would be likely to happen. Somewhat late in the day, the well-meaning inspector told them that people in the court would try and upset them, confuse them and make them angry. They might possibly even make them out to be liars. But, he assured them, as long as they stuck to the truth, and the stories they had already told, everything would be fine. That last-minute pep talk in no way prepared the girls for what was to follow.

As Donna entered the courtroom she saw a sea of unfamiliar faces. Some of them were wearing wigs and black gowns. She had not been told about that. She did not know who was her barrister, and nobody told her. She recognized only two people – her father, dressed in a brown tweed suit and flamboyant tie, who looked at her intently, and the social worker, who was in the public gallery. She was equally unprepared for the formal language and appearance of the judge. Her first replies were barely audible. She was on the witness stand for three hours. Donna found it was a difficult story to tell.

She was cross-examined minutely on the occasions of abuse that she had outlined to the police. The first occasion she had described was when she had sat next to her father on the sofa. She knew it was just after her birthday. But she could not clearly remember whether it was her seventh or eighth birthday. Either way it was eight or nine years ago. But defence counsel remarked on the curious lapse of memory. He suggested that other events she had apparently remembered might not be accurate.

Donna's recollections became more and more vague. Defence counsel asked her if her father 'had ever had intercourse with us. I didn't know what to do and I just burst out crying. Because I didn't know what to say because there were all these fellers round and my dad was straight over the other side. I were that shaken,' she told us a few months later. None of the laborious statements the police had taken could be used in court. Donna had to tell the story in her own words and outline the allegations. Her evidence, although consistent, was vague.

Defence counsel then moved on to Donna's relationship with her father. It was true she had not got on well with him. It was also true that in the last year when she had been living with him, after her mother had left, she had run away from home several times. Counsel then put it to her that she was trying to get back at her father because he forbade her to go out with her boyfriend. And at this point he produced a letter from her boyfriend and read out to the court extracts that had sexual connotations. The implication was clear. She was no sexual innocent. She was asked point-blank whether in fact she had had sexual relations. The court was left in no doubt. Donna was devastated. She still remembers that as the worst incident in the courtroom. The focus had changed. It was she who was on trial.

The jury who watched this cross-examination must have been less than clear. Donna went through a range of emotions. She was shy, at the beginning. She became angry at the way the questions implied her own lack of morality. She burst into tears at one point and when she recovered, to save her own face, she became somewhat truculent. What particularly irritated her was an accusation that the men coming to call on her mother were in fact coming to see her.

Her sister Shelley was given an even harder time. She turned up in court wearing jeans and sneakers. She looked small and younger than her twelve years. The judge asked her if she knew the difference between truth and lies, and asked her what she thought the truth was. She replied that it was not telling lies. The judge then went on to question her on whether she understood what an oath was. She replied that it was a serious promise to tell the truth. The court was then stood down and little Shelley was left with the prosecuting barrister who asked her a few more questions about truth and lies. She began to be confused. She could barely understand his accent and he had difficulty with her broad brogue. After a short break, the barrister conferred with the judge who decided that Shelley was not able to give evidence on oath. That meant she could not swear on the Bible to tell 'the whole truth and nothing but the truth', but she was allowed to give evidence unsworn. If the jury were to rely on her testimony, it had to be corroborated – that is, there had to be something or someone to confirm her story. Counsel for the defence nonetheless cross-questioned her very closely. The prosecution was relying on her to corroborate her sister's account of the early incident on the sofa. Predictably she was vague about this. And defence counsel put it to her that her sister had influenced her and forced her to make up that story. Shelley hesitated and then dissolved into tears. The court waited. The social worker tried to get near to comfort her but was firmly told to be seated. Shelley never regained her composure. She related the two incidents she had told to the police. But no one had seen either of these take place and as she was uncorroborated the allegations were dismissed. After the trial she broke down and wept convulsively for hours. No one was able to console her. Today she refuses to talk about the trial or her father.

The father spoke in his own defence and denied all the charges. He was calm throughout. Although not a tall man, he was very well built. His florid face gave the impression of someone who liked to drink. He spoke in low tones, gazing calmly at the questioners.  He told the court how he blamed himself for denying the children a proper homelife. His wife had left, and he felt full of remorse. He loved his children and would never have done anything to harm them. He had shown them the same physical affection that any loving father would. Yes, he liked the odd drink, but then what man didn't? He had had two previous convictions but they were for petty theft; there had never been any suggestion of anything odd sexually. He currently had a very attractive girlfriend. She had no complaints.

He dealt with the various allegations without too much difficulty. He had at times put his arm round his daughter, and perhaps hugged her. But he was a large man and quite strong and his arm may have stretched a little further than he imagined. He admitted getting into bed with Donna and lying next to her, to comfort her. But he had not taken his trousers off or clambered on top of her.

Derek also appeared to be sympathetic to his daughter. He claimed he understood why it was that Donna felt so aggrieved. But he hastened to add she was a difficult girl to control, quite headstrong. He had done his best with her. He had confessed originally to spare the girls the ordeal of a trial, to protect them. It had all been a terrible shock.

The paediatrician was called and she gave her medical evidence. She gave the opinion that both girls appeared to have experienced sexual abuse and was questioned quite closely about how she had arrived at such a conclusion. Of course, with the twelve-year-old she could claim that it was most unusual. With Donna it was less clear. She was not allowed to tell the court what the girls had told her. She stated that, in her long experience in these matters, her opinion based on the medical evidence was that the girls had been abused. Her statements about Shelley were not taken into account: even if it were accepted that Shelley had experienced penetration there was no proof that it was her father. And the evidence on Donna was muddied by what the jury had learned of her sexual exploits.

The mother was briefly called and disposed of quite efficiently by the defence. Although it was claimed that Donna had told her what her father was doing, it was made quite clear that her mother did not get on well with Donna or her father. There were glimpses of the other side of the story as she described the stormy, violent marriage and her husband's drinking problem. But she was not allowed to elaborate very much on that. She had abandoned her children to their father and set up house with a new man. So it could hardly be alleged that she was worried about what Derek was doing to his children. She too left the witness stand in tears.

The trial took three days. At the end the judge directed the jury to ignore the unsworn testimony of the younger child, as it was uncorroborated. He outlined Donna's sexual experience and her poor relationship with her father, and the suggestion that the two girls may have been colluding against their father in a bid to gain their revenge on him. It was not clear whether that was supposedly to do with their mother leaving or the girls being jealous of their father's new girlfriend. The allegations that had been made were vague, and Donna's memory unclear. The police had admitted that the father had initially confessed after many hours of questioning when he was very tired and angry. The testimony from the one independent witness, the paediatrician, was not entirely clear. She had claimed that medically the younger child exhibited signs consistent with penetration. But it was difficult to ascertain whether in fact that was a result of sexual abuse. Finally he warned the jury that in order to convict they had to be sure that the accused was guilty.

The father was acquitted.

When we spoke to Donna a few months later the court experience was a bad memory. She had been quite enthusiastic about putting her father's exploits on the record when she had gone to the social services originally. But that had been nine months earlier. By the time she came to court she had begun to put the whole thing behind her. She had a new life with a new family and had not seen her father or mother for months. She found having to drag up all the old memories in court unbearably painful. 'I don't know what I said,' she recalled later, 'because I were too upset to say anything. I just stood there dazed. And when you're that upset and specially seeing your mum who abandoned you with a new husband, you don't know what to say to the barristers, because you don't know what they're going to ask you so your mind goes blank. And you're that upset to say anything, you just cry, and that's what I did.'

She found it difficult to reply to specific questions, not just because the atmosphere was so formal and apparently hostile – although that was bad enough – but more because the acts and events she was asked to describe were very private. She had spoken of them hardly at all and had kept them buried inside her for years. When she had arrived on the social worker's doorstep she had burst out with most of her accusations. Later the police had coaxed more details from her but that had not been easy. In court, however, faced with these strange faces, with her father staring at her from the corner, she found the story difficult to tell. She could not understand why they did not believe her. Up till then the adults who had listened to her had believed her and supported her. When she heard the verdict she was puzzled and angry. Limply she kept saying to us, 'He should have been punished for what he'd done, he should have got some, they should have believed us.'

Donna came out of court feeling that her father had wrecked her life and her sister's and he would never have to pay for it. She feels betrayed not only by him but by the social workers and police who promised her justice. Most of all she feels unsure about the whole episode. She has a sneaking feeling that, despite her own strong disgust and fear at what her father did to her, perhaps it was her fault somewhere. She nurses a secret fear that perhaps the court decision was right. But she knows she did not imagine the years of sexual abuse. She lives with a consuming passion for revenge. 'One day I'll kill him', she told us, adding as an afterthought, as she is now a born-again Christian, 'God will show me the way.'

The central problem, as one lawyer explained, 'can be described in one word – corroboration. That's the top and bottom of it.' Even though her story was taken seriously enough to put her into care, there was not enough evidence in the legal sense to prove beyond all reasonable doubt that her father was guilty. In law, where the charge concerns a sexual offence, the judge should warn the jury of acting on the uncorroborated evidence, although they can act on that evidence if they are convinced that the witness is telling the truth. Corroboration is something or someone that confirms the girl's story. Witnesses would be ideal, but the only witnesses to what had gone on were the two girls. They had slept in the same bedroom and each had heard and seen the father crawling into the other's bed. They had never discussed it with each other before the court case. It was a secret both of them kept to themselves.

The police had hoped that Shelley would provide the corroboration on one story and be a witness herself. Unfortunately she was unable to provide a clear enough account of the event she had witnessed when she was very small. Although she was much clearer about the abuse in the last two years the judge directed the jury to disregard her evidence: an unsworn testimony has to be corroborated. It made little difference that the paediatrician had medical evidence; in the circumstances that proved nothing. And, as it turned out, poor Shelley became more of a liability than an asset. The defence suggested collusion, rather than corroboration. Shelley could not argue back. The jury may well have thought she accepted the charge.

The judge decides whether the child is old enough or intelligent enough to understand the implications of taking the oath. The court can accept the unsworn evidence of a child if he or she has 'sufficient intelligence' and understands the duty of speaking the truth. But no one can be convicted on that evidence alone. Shelley found the whole experience far worse than standing up in the middle of class trying to remember her homework. And it was not a topic she relished talking about in the first place. She was distraught because she had lost her mother and had tried to see her on several occasions without much success, so she was loath to lose her father too by accusing him publicly of mistreating her. As Donna recalled, 'She were terrified. I were terrified but I knew I could go through with it. But I knew she couldn't go through with it. I knew when she saw me dad's face she would just cry and she wouldn't speak to anyone.'

Shelley was twelve at the time. If her evidence was considered unreliable, what are the chances of prosecution with children who are much younger? Certainly a five-, six- or seven-year-old could not possibly be expected to conceptualize truth and lies. And that is an age at which abuse frequently occurs. At that age children cannot legitimately take the witness stand and appear credible, so many cases remain unprosecuted. The paediatrician Jane Wynne described a current case with a four-year-old who had been brought in with considerable damage to her anal passage. Using dolls that have adult sexual parts, the child explained and clearly demonstrated what her stepfather had done to her. Outraged, the paediatrician tried to get him brought to justice. But the Director of Public Prosecutions felt there was not enough evidence to prosecute. No witness, no corroboration, just the unsworn testimony of a four-year-old. No chance.

In Donna's case there were no other witnesses. But witnesses in this type of case are notoriously difficult to find. Like rape, child sexual abuse does not take place publicly, but in the darkness in bedrooms, living rooms, in private, secret places.

Donna's mother had been told about things at home but had not seen anything. The social worker had been told, so had the paediatrician and the police. But none of them had seen anything and their evidence was only hearsay. Hearsay evidence is not allowed in British courts. In America the difficulties of finding witnesses for this type of crime have been recognized and hearsay evidence is allowed, particularly from professionals who can also describe the child's physical and emotional state at the time of questioning.

The jury was left to decide in this case on Donna's testimony. Clearly, if the burden of proof is to be put on girls like Donna or Shelley, some thought has to be given to the difficulties of court appearances. They are frightening enough for an adult. For a child they are considerably worse. Courts are designed to be formal, daunting, authoritative places. The costumes of barristers and judges are supposed to bestow on their wearers an aura of dignity and give them a special status. They look different from the others because of their wigs and gowns, they sound different because of their own curious language, and they act differently because they understand the rituals of the courtroom. The ordinary people, who appear as themselves with no fancy dress, are clearly at a disadvantage. If those people are children who do not understand either the formality or the language, they have an even greater disadvantage.

Until the day of the court hearing Donna and Shelley had been listened to quite sympathetically by adults. They had been questioned in a normal conversational way. They had been given time to answer. The interviews were designed to help them clarify their experience. The people who talked to them were supportive. Above all the girls were believed.

The courtroom experience turned out to be almost the opposite of that. Neither of the girls had spoken to or met their barrister before the trial. They did not fully understand what the barristers were trying to do. Neither of them was told what they would undergo as players in an adversarial battle. One hour before their appearance they were given a briefing on cross-examination and told what might happen to them. By then they were far too anxious and nervous to absorb the information. So they were quite unprepared for the ordeal they were put through. No matter how clear the girls had been in their interviews before, it was what they said in court that mattered. Prosecution lawyers cannot read out their statements or suggest events to them to try and jog their memories. That would be leading the witness. So if the witnesses are too tongue-tied to talk, no one can fill in the gaps. And that is partly what happened. For example, Donna was too confused to mention in court that she had slept in the top bunk at the time in question. Derek was not a tall man, and it would have been quite an effort for him to have climbed into her bed. He described the incident in court as if he'd just popped into the bed without thinking and without any effort.

When Donna talked to us later it took some time before she told her story. At the beginning she denied everything: she was inarticulate and vague, yet she was clear about her father's violence. In talking about him she vacillated. One minute he was loving and good. The next he was punitive and drunken. The main thrust of her story, when she finally poured it out, was difficult to doubt. It was the details that made it come alive. In the last year she recalled, 'He got into bed with us and he did have sex with me in a way but not in the way like men have sex with you. Like he put his penis inside but he just laid there, not moving in and out like men do. And that were it ...'

Clearly if cases like this are to remain within the criminal justice system, and if there is some intention of bringing these offenders to justice, child witnesses have to be better prepared or the system has to change to adjust to new needs. At the moment the law bends over backwards in favour of the defendant rather than the child. The promise of videos could change that a little.

A video recording would have been a distinct advantage in Donna and Shelley's case. Their story was slow to emerge and was vague. The paediatrician, who is equipped with a video and raring to go, only did a twenty-minute interview with each of the girls and they told her more in that time than they had told the social workers or the police. In court they were even briefer. By that time they had been settled in a foster-home for nine months and found it difficult to remember in detail the statements they had made to the police. The formal and uneasy court atmosphere did not help.

The advantages would be greater for even younger children. Often they are only prepared to tell their story once. Child specialists have often despaired that a child who was quite explicit in a first interview will refuse to repeat the story. It is often too painful to tell twice. And from a child's point of view, once it has been said, there is no sense in saying it again and again. The allegations that were taped would have to be the very first ones.

In Texas video evidence is allowed in court and it has been found to provide an extra bonus. The law was changed in August 1983 to allow a taped interview of the child's testimony in court. In that interview neither prosecuting nor defence lawyers are present. The child is taken through the events fairly briskly by a professional police interviewer. The tape is shown to the person charged and the net result is that over 85 per cent plead guilty before the case ever gets to court. This saves the court's time and saves the child from an ordeal.

It would be a mistake to think that video evidence is a complete solution. For a start there is the slight problem of unsworn evidence. In Texas the State prosecution dismiss this with barely a backward glance: 'An oath is no guarantee of trustworthiness by any witness – a good percent of sworn witnesses lie anyway. Children of tender years who cannot reason abstractly and cannot qualify to take an oath should still be allowed to relate how they were abused – what factually happened – an ability they may possess.'

But even in Texas it appears that most prosecutors and most juries would still prefer to call the child as a witness if they feel that he or she can handle the experience. Certainly defence lawyers believe that the defendant has the right in law to face his accuser and will argue to that effect. But the Texans have even devised a way around that. If the child is brought into court, and has to be cross-examined, this can be done in a private room on video and be simultaneously broadcast to the judge and jury in court. It is not clear whether that is less traumatic for the child than being in the courtroom. Clearly the child does not have to face the alleged perpetrator, but he or she does have to undergo cross-questioning and has to be well prepared in order to do that.

Since its introduction in Texas most of the trial cases that have used tape have resulted in a conviction. But then as the Texans themselves note almost in passing, 'The State wins most of the cases tried to a jury and the video tape will probably not affect the percentage won. It will make some cases prosecutable that would otherwise be dismissed.'

So how will the experiment travel? It could be that the tape revolution, if it gets under way, will enable more cases to go to court. It may also produce more pleas of guilty.

Successful tape interviews could solve a number of problems. But there is still the vexing question of corroboration. There is the inadmissibility of hearsay evidence. If, as the defence lawyers will undoubtedly argue, the child should face the defendant, then the child witness must be better prepared for court.

Once again, American experiments lead the way. Ten years ago when the size of the problem began to be recognized, experiments were set up in five states. Some states tried the video experiment and moved on. Most of them have made quite radical changes. In Seattle, Washington, Donna and Shelley would have had a completely different experience. There the system has been adapted to take into account the rights of the child. It has become axiomatic that even if the child does not understand the law he or she must still be protected by the law. All the lawyers and judges go on training courses to learn how to talk to children, to understand their language and intellectual development. It is emphasized that the child will tell the story best to someone he or she knows. Great pains are taken to ensure that the child builds a relationship with the prosecuting lawyer who stays with him or her from the beginning to the end of a case. It is the prosecuting lawyer who first interviews the child, and sees him or her frequently before the case goes to court. The child is taken into the court and shown what happens. Everything is done to make him or her feel as confident as possible. That is clearly in the interest of the prosecution, as well as of the child.

Because the children are well prepared, they tend to be very credible witnesses. Children of four, five and six routinely testify and perform well in court even when the defence tried to discredit their story. The State attorney's department makes no secret of the fact that prosecutions tend to be successful. There is a sensible logic to that. Defendants realize that if the case does go to court they are likely to lose. So there is strong pressure on them to plead guilty. Plea bargaining and treatment are used as added incentives to get a guilty plea. As a consequence over three-quarters of the defendants plead guilty and never go to court.

Once the cases do go to court they are tried slightly differently from that of Donna and Shelley. True, the children are subject to the same cross-examination as they would be in England. The defence would be concerned to discredit the child's story. But the child would be much more relaxed. He or she would know the prosecuting lawyer very well, and would understand the questions. The courtroom itself would be far less intimidating and no one would be wearing wigs. Above all the child would be asked questions by someone who had been trained in talking to children. So the child would be likely to answer clearly even though the defendant was in court.

Corroboration is not considered necessary. The case could well stand or fall on the evidence of one child alone. Hearsay evidence is allowed if the child testifies. So someone who has heard the story from the child can also testify, once the child has taken the stand. All sorts of experts can be wheeled in to support the case. Child development specialists can offer evidence about the child's behaviour which would support the statements.

Experts can be called to forestall difficult cross-examination of the child. If for example the defence questions the child about why he or she took so long to reveal the offence, an expert can testify that this would be perfectly normal behaviour in a child because most children would not instantly talk of something as traumatic as this. Or, to take another example which would be all too familiar to Donna, experts can be brought in to testify on a child's memory. They could explain what was and was not likely to be remembered, and how far back a child could normally recall events. They can, in the case of unsworn children, be asked to give evidence on truth-telling. Above all, they can be called upon if the prosecution considers that an issue is being raised improperly. No doubt such experts would have had a field day had they been present when Donna's sexuality was discussed. Certainly no one in the English court suggested that the daughter's sexuality had any connection with the defendant. Someone in Seattle would most certainly have considered that worthy of note.

Curiously, no consideration seems to have been given to adapting the English legal system to the new explosion in child-abuse cases. And yet children who go through the juvenile system, where they themselves face criminal charges, get far better treatment. The court is made as informal as possible. The public are not admitted. There is no jury. The child is questioned with a view to deciding what is best for him or her in the future. Yet a child who is only a witness in a criminal court, not a defendant, will get none of these benefits.

One of the biggest changes that some American states have made is in their treatment of the victims and potential witnesses. As soon as any child is thought to have been abused he or she is immediately put into a therapy programme. Initially this lasts for 6 weeks, but it could take much longer. Research has shown that those who have themselves been abused are likely to become abusers themselves, and great pains are taken to break that cycle. In England most of us seem to be unaware of that problem.

Six months after their traumatic court case, Donna and Shelley have received practical help. They are comfortably installed in a foster-home and discuss school work and practical problems with their hard-pressed social worker. But no one considers it useful or necessary to do any more. Shelley has begun to regress and now has friends who are at least three or four years younger than her. She often breaks into babytalk. Donna frequently hears her sobbing at night, but knows she will not talk about anything. Donna is convinced that her sister will never marry or have babies: 'She's that terrified of men.' Donna veers between wild bouts of promiscuity and virginal if not completely frigid relationships. She can barely read or write, so her chances of finding a good job are small. Her conclusion is chilling: 'My father has put us in a prison because of what he did to us. He's wrecked our lives. He's ruined us. We can never lead normal lives me and me sister because of what he's done to us. And he's out there free as a bird.'

# 6  LISTENING TO THE CHILDREN

One of the problems that plagues those dealing with child sexual abuse is that the physical evidence can be ambiguous; the only explicit evidence is the child's account of what happened. Children who have been hit or subjected to physical mistreatment have fractures, bruises, cuts, burn marks, which can be diagnosed fairly readily. x-rays can be carried out, patients can be hospitalized and the symptoms can be treated. In the early 1960s the medical profession, particularly paediatricians, began to realize the enormous medical and social implications of abuse, and so they began to develop as an important pressure group. Before long, other professionals and policy-makers started to take it very seriously. But they have been slower to recognize sexual abuse. It has no clear medical component, it is difficult to diagnose and even more difficult to treat. Above all it requires believing in a child, rather than scientific examination, and doctors are not comfortable in that role. Traditionally that is the work of psychiatrists.

Psychiatrists have long had access to the secret and private world of children, but they have been very slow to focus on sexual abuse, largely because their profession has been, and still is, fraught with ambivalence about children's truthfulness.

Historically, Freud must take a great deal of the blame for this. He had several patients who claimed to have been sexually abused, and in 1896 he wrote a paper on the causes of neurosis which was based on the experiences of thirteen patients, all of whom had been abused as children. He did not use the term

This drawing was made by a twelve-year-old girl who had
been subjected to sexual abuse by an uncle living in her
home. At the time she was still in a phase of such terror
that she was unable to speak to her psychotherapist and
could manage only to draw.

The picture itself has a nightmarish quality of helpless
entrapment within a web of suddenly changing
perspectives. It is not clear whether she is lying on a bed
or in a coffin; she seems like only a shred of a person,
more like a soundless scream. The man, in contrast,
appears very large, indifferent and content.

(This picture was kindly supplied by the Child and
Family Department of the Tavistock Clinic.)

'abuse' but one with slightly more romantic overtones, 'seduction', though there was no doubt that the act he was describing was the same. He wrote: 'It was represented either by a brutal assault committed by an adult or by a seduction less rapid and less repulsive but reaching the same conclusion.' He argued that it was these childhood events that had contributed to the patients' neuroses. He assumed that if his theory were correct then sexual abuse was both far more important than anyone had realized up till then and far more widespread.

Freud was convinced that the patients were not lying about their earlier experiences and that the events could not be written off as hysterical ramblings. He spent hours with them and felt the stories they had remembered were very real. None of the patients had told him initially what had happened to them. Their memories had begun to surface only after hours of questioning. They had repressed their experiences for years and found it extremely painful to talk about them. Freud found that the only way the patients could unlock the past was by intensive treatment. He explained:

> One only succeeds in awakening the psychical trace of a precocious sexual event under the most energetic pressure of the analytic procedure and against enormous resistance. Moreover the memory must be extracted from them piece by piece, and while it is being awakened in their unconscious they become prey to an emotion which it would be hard to counterfeit.

The paper he published sent shock-waves through the psychological and medical world of contemporary Vienna. His colleagues closed ranks and universally condemned him. A typical reaction came from a fellow psychiatrist, Conrad Rieger, who wrote:

> I cannot believe that an experienced psychiatrist can read this paper without experiencing genuine outrage. The reason for this outrage is to be found in the fact that Freud takes very seriously what is nothing but paranoid drivel with a sexual content – purely chance events – which are entirely insignificant or entirely invented.

Isolated, and at odds with the rigid Victorian morality of his Viennese colleagues, Freud began to question his own findings. Over the next few years he decided that the research he had done and the conclusion he had reached had been mistaken. He did a complete and extraordinary intellectual about-turn and (according to the latest research by Jeffrey Masson) he retracted his theory completely, concluding that most of the 'seductions' which his patients had revealed had never occurred at all. They had not been 'brutally assaulted' or 'repulsively seduced' as he had thought, they had merely imagined it. Instead of adults, or more particularly fathers, wanting to seduce their children, it was the children who had imagined the aggression and indeed often secretly invited it. From that it was only one step to developing his theory of the Oedipus complex, which assumed that every child at a certain stage of development actively wants to be seduced by his or her parent and often imagines that it has happened.

The Oedipus complex placed a convenient smokescreen between fantasy and reality. If children dreamed of sexual relations with their parents, all allegations could be written off as normal fantasy. There was certainly no need to take the accusations seriously. Indeed Freud himself allowed that there was no distinction between the two. In 1916 he wrote: 'If in the case of girls who produce such an event [seduction] in their story of their childhood their father figures regularly as the seducer then there can be no doubt either of the imaginary nature of the accusation or of the motive that has led to it.'

Thanks to Freud's influence a generation of psychiatrists were trained to react to stories about sexual abuse by assuming it was fantasy. Real memories of traumas experienced were not taken very seriously since it was assumed that whether it was real or imagined the effect was the same. So presumably hundreds or thousands of patients were left completely confused about reality and fantasy. If their real experiences were not treated seriously it showed a complete disregard for their own integrity and for the importance of their own experiences. It does not require very much imagination to see what further damage that could do to a patient already traumatized.

The Oedipal theory also managed very neatly to shift all the responsibility on to the child victim and away from the parents or 'seducer'. Florence Rush, a scholarly feminist writer, poign-antly explored this effect in an article in 1977 called 'The Freud-ian Cover-Up':

> The seduction theory maintained that hysteria was a neurosis caused by sexual assault, and it incriminated incestuous fathers, while the Oedipal theory insisted that the seduction was a fantasy, an invention, not a fact – and it incriminated daughters. . . . However, one must remember that when Freud arrived at the seduction theory he did so by listening carefully and intently to his female patients; when he arrived at his Oedipal theory, he did so by listening carefully and intently to himself. . . . Freud cautioned the world never to overestimate the importance of seduction and the world listened to Freud and paid little heed to the sexual abuse of children. . . . The reason is illogical. It categorically assigns a real experience to fantasy, or harmless reality at best, while the known offender, the one concrete reality, is ignored. With reality sacrificed to a nebulous unconscious, the little girl has no recourse. She is trapped within a web of adult conjecture and is not offered protection but treatment for some speculative ailment, while the offender – Uncle Willie, the grocery clerk, the dentist or the little girl's father – is permitted to indulge his predilection for little girls. The child's experience is as terrifying as the worst Kafkaesque nightmare: her story is not believed, she is declared ill and, worse, she is left at the mercy and the 'benevolence' of psychiatrically oriented child experts.

The professionals who were in the best position to learn about incest and sexual family secrets ignored what they heard, and many continue to do so.

Today some members of the psychiatric profession are less hidebound by the limitations of Freudian concepts but even they are only just beginning to come to terms with the scale of a problem that Freud himself originally uncovered. Psychiatrists who work with children are leading the way. This in itself is a breakthrough. It has been endlessly reiterated in past research studies that children do not tell the truth, are very suggestible and have poor memories. All the evidence points, in fact, to the opposite.

The largest study on children's truthfulness comes from Seattle, Washington, where there has been a Treatment Assault programme since the 1970s. The medical director of the programme, a paediatrician, Dr Shirley Cooke Anderson, has monitored its results since 1973. There have been 2,000 reported assaults each year, of which 1,200 are perpetrated on children. So in the last few years the team has had as much experience as anyone in the world. Their results show that less than 2 per cent of the stories that the children tell prove to be false. Those very few children who make up stories are normally older, emotionally disturbed, or caught up in custody disputes, and the reasons for their lies are obvious almost immediately.

In Britain, those who have most experience with abused children come to the same conclusions as the researchers in the US, and tend to believe the children's stories. The most influential work has stemmed from the psychiatric unit attached to the large children's hospital, Great Ormond Street in London. A child-abuse unit was set up in 1981 to treat children known to have been sexually abused, and to assist their families. In five years it has dealt with over 500 cases and it is currently finding it almost impossible to deal with the increased demand from social services departments and the medical profession. What began as a treatment centre has expanded into a place where children are sent by schools and social services agencies to confirm a suspected sexual abuse. With these referrals the therapists carry out what they call 'disclosure' interviews to determine whether or not a child can be said to have been abused. The unit has become the pioneer in Britain for both the detection and the treatment of child sexual abuse.

Dr Arnon Bentovim, the founding father of the unit, had this to say about the children he sees: 'We have had a notion up till recent years that what children are telling us are their wishes, their fantasies, what they'd like to happen – not what actually happens. But I think now we are recognizing that a significant number of children do have such experiences. So basically we feel we believe it, as long as we get the picture from the child.'

Years of clinical practice have hardened the unit to acts that would be beyond most people's fantasies. After the initial shock of discovering what adults could actually do to children they have learned how to talk to children and how to listen to them to ease them through their stories. Direct questioning with younger children under seven is often a very poor way of getting information. Dr Eileen Vizard, who worked at the unit, recalled, 'Some children cannot simply tell their story. Direct questioning may elicit a frozen blank stare or silence, like a four-year-old electively mute child with gonorrhoea I saw, who tore clumps of her hair out and said nothing in my diagnostic interview. Only after two years of play therapy elsewhere was this little girl able to describe her abuse in words and with anatomical dolls. Similarly, premature direct questioning may push a frightened child into blurting out a denial of abuse which may then make the child feel overwhelmed with hopelessness and cause further withdrawal.'

At the unit the staff have learned to adapt the interview technique to the way children respond. One of the methods that they have developed in the last two years is a style of play therapy using dolls. These dolls are specially made and have all the adult sexual parts. They make the children undress the dolls and look at the various parts. Then they ask them what their own terms are for all the different body parts. They set up a family which corresponds to that of the child, so there might be a mummy doll and a daddy doll and, say, a 'Jane' doll. The interview is conducted in a deliberately relaxed way to set the children as much at ease as possible and to get them to talk about the possible physical connections between the doll family. It has proved to be an extremely effective way of getting younger children to describe their experiences.

Children will often graphically demonstrate sexual acts using the dolls. They can place one doll on top of the other to show how an act took place, and they can explain masturbation and oral sex in a way that would be impossible with their own limited vocabulary. It also allows them to distance themselves from the act. The more bizarre the events which the children recount or demonstrate, the more the psychiatrists are inclined to accept the children's story. Dr Vizard explained to us: 'I think we would feel that this is not information which is readily available to ordinary children and that it is information which results from a pattern of experience of sexual abuse. And I think that we would certainly want to believe that child's allegations, because we know of the awful consequences of not believing children and we know the things which can affect adult incest victims in later life.'

Even then interviewers at the unit have to coax the child to talk about such secret matters, and they often have to exert some pressure in order to make the child talk. It is very rare indeed that children will spontaneously talk about things which have been done to them over a long period of time and which have been kept quite secret. Dr Bentovim told us of a case he saw recently. A small girl had been repeatedly interviewed about possible abuse, and she had consistently avoided answering. After several weeks she suddenly and spontaneously demonstrated with the dolls how her father had sexually abused her. Somewhat surprised, Dr Bentovim asked her why she had not told him that before. She replied, 'Well, I can tell you now because my dad's dead, isn't he?' Her father had indeed died one week earlier. At last she felt free to tell.

Few children find it easy to tell. They are caught up in a confusion of conflicting loyalties. Sexual abuse within the family is always secret, so telling means getting someone into trouble. Many children are threatened with all manner of punishments if they do tell. Others may be faced with parents who deny everything. Perhaps saddest of all, there are children who may see it as the only form of affection they receive in a hopelessly bleak world and are loath to let go of that too. One seven-year-old boy had been brought to Great Ormond Street because his mother had seen him attempting sexual intercourse with his baby sister. He was a very disturbed child, almost inarticulate. He answered most questions by a nod or shake of his head, or by using the dolls. Then, because research at the unit has repeatedly shown that abusers of siblings are frequently the victims of abuse themselves, the interview took a different turn. They began to ask the boy whether he himself had had sexual intercourse. He agreed that he had. It was suggested that he had been abused by his father. At first he rejected this, but when he was asked it again in a slightly different way, using the dolls, he identified the doll abusing him as his father. The interview continued and the psychiatrists were quite sure at the end that the boy had been a victim of quite severe abuse for many years.

His parents, who had vehemently denied ever doing anything to the child, were waiting for him when he came out of the interview room. When the poor bewildered boy saw them he broke down in tears and said he had done nothing. Sobbing, he cried out to his parents, 'They made me say it. My dad is my mate,' and rushed towards them. They were astonished, frozen, and continued to deny everything. For that child, even the most unwanted assault by his father may have been preferable to an empty world without attention and love. So it was perhaps not surprising that he wanted to deny everything, to forget it, to blot it out.

Because so many of the children who come to the unit are in some conflict about telling, the unit has developed particular techniques. Dr Vizard explained to us, 'For those children who may be under a great deal of emotional pressure and who find it actually impossible to share the details of their abuse without help from us, we have developed a technique of questioning which I think helps to ensure that the child is not allowed to become stuck in conflict and is helped to continue on to the next question and hopefully eventually to share what has happened to them.'

All this would have had a familiar ring to Freud, in the early days before he retracted. It is worth noting again that he wrote: 'One only succeeds ... under the most energetic pressure of the analytic procedure and against enormous resistance.' And this was with adults who have far less to fear than children.

The interview technique which the Great Ormond Street team have evolved was originally intended for therapeutic purposes where abuse was admitted or powerfully corroborated. Dr Bentovim told us: 'Because we are clinicians we're not really thinking in terms of a confession, but we are thinking in terms of helping a child to make a disclosure about being sexually abused, from the point of view of achieving some therapeutic relief for that child. And it's terribly important that those deeds are spelled out in some way in the interview so we can work out the best form of child care. Until we know what has happened we can't be sure how much and to what extent we need to protect the child.'

The interviews are often long and deliberately unstructured. They are always recorded on video tape. Bentovim said, 'This forms part of our case-notes.' And the unit examines not just what the child is saying. The staff note how the child responds to the different questions, when he or she shows signs of anxiety, at what point he or she appears to withdraw and so on. In one interview we were shown, the therapist pointed out how the child gradually exhibited more and more disturbed behaviour as she began to reveal what had been happening. On another tape, a four-year-old girl was being questioned in the same room as her older brother and sister. They had both described a long list of abuse. The therapist was trying to discover whether the youngest child had had a similar experience. At first she denied everything and shook her head vehemently. We did not immediately notice the reactions of her brother and sister when she had shaken her head. The expert team played it back to us and showed us that each time the little girl had denied it, her brother and sister had looked at each other slyly and smiled. At the end of half an hour the four-year-old did in fact spell out quite a number of hideous acts that her father had performed. The brother curled up more and more as he listened. The other sister became hyperactive. When the father entered at the end of the tape and was confronted with the information he flatly denied it all. In this case, the psychiatrists believed the child, not the father.

Bentovim is convinced that the video recording is an invaluable tool in making decisions about what should be done in the best interests of the child. Once he and his team are clear about what has been happening in the family they organize the social services, the health service and possibly the community police to arrange the best outcome for that child.

The Great Ormond Street unit's influence on current thinking has been extensive. The most recent DHSS guidelines (*Child Abuse – Working Together*, 1986) insist that a child making an allegation of sexual abuse should be believed until proved incorrect.

Unfortunately this view is almost diametrically opposed to that of the legal profession. Lawyers have always been keen to emphasize that their accused client is innocent until proved guilty and the corollary of that often means that the accusing child is lying until proved correct.

It is hardly surprising that when psychiatrists confront lawyers there is a certain amount of dispute. The law is looking for clear-cut answers, true or false. Lawyers want to cross-examine in a simple, direct way. Psychiatrists have learned to talk to children slowly and gently to overcome embarrassment; they often exert pressure to prevent the children from clamming up altogether; they tend to ask questions over and over again to overcome repression and fear, and they use dolls and suggestions to make them tell their stories.

Psychiatrists like those at Great Ormond Street believe that you cannot treat children's evidence in the same way as that of an adult. Adults have such a wide variety of experiences, and have aquired the appropriate vocabulary to describe them. Children's experience is limited, and their vocabulary even more so. If they do not know about sexual acts or why people perform them, then those acts are difficult to understand and explain. One child described her abuse as 'grandpa trying to do some push-ups on top of me'. Another little girl remembered the smile on the face of her stepfather as he masturbated and could barely recall what his hand was doing.

By an unfortunate twist of fate, the work of the unit is causing mayhem in the High Court in a way that was never intended. Many children who come to the unit end up in the High Court, mostly on wardship cases. These proceedings are not criminal, but are brought to enable the court to decide what is in 'the best interests of the child'. In wardship proceedings, if the judge learns that a video has been made, he will want to see it, and so will all the other interested parties in the court. Representatives of the parties concerned will watch the recorded interview and will come to their own conclusions about both the truthfulness of the child and the reliability of the interview. What began as an extra clinical tool to be interpreted with other case-notes by experienced clinicians suddenly undergoes the full rigour of the court process. Completely unplanned, in that quaint way we British have of embracing new ideas, videos have been dragged in through the back door to serve a purpose that was never intended. As a consequence both the methods used by the Great Ormond Street unit and their interpretation of children's behaviour are being severely hammered. Unfavourable headlines appear, such as 'Videotaped interviews in child-abuse cases criticized by judge'.

A recent and fairly typical case that went to the High Court in the summer of 1986 brought into conflict two fundamental principles of the two professions: the need to obtain the truth from the child and the requirement of natural justice for the parents. The two principles are conventionally thought to be in harmony, but abused children, as we have seen, tend not to make statements against their parents unless they are put under some pressure and asked fairly hypothetical questions. To compound that difficulty, the investigation is often carried out without the parents' knowledge to ensure that they do not frighten the child into silence. Thus there is an element of what one judge has called 'suppressed truth, sometimes even deception' in the methods used to obtain some evidence. In this particular case the psychiatrists were convinced that the child was telling the truth about her own abuse, despite the fact that her parents hotly denied it. The parents were in fact horrified at the mere suggestion. This is not apparently unusual. Parents often lie to save themselves, but they can also blot out or repress what has happened because they feel ashamed or guilty. Left to themselves the unit might have been able to work out a solution for the child. Once it gets to court the problem takes on a different dimension.

The case involved a five-year-old girl, Annie. Her father was forty-five and was employed in middle management as area manager for a firm of retail food stores. Annie was the eldest daughter of his second marriage. He had had four children by his first wife, ranging in age from twenty-two to fifteen. He had met his current wife at work – she was an employee in the same firm. When he first began his association with her she was nineteen, only three years older than his eldest daughter. He married her a few days after Annie was born. Two years later they had a second little girl.

The father worked long hours, which meant that he often left the house before the girls were awake and arrived home after they had gone to sleep. When he was there he tried to involve himself with the girls, changing their nappies, helping to feed them and so on. The household was one the judge described as 'modest', by which he meant one where 'nakedness by adults is regarded as unseemly, and where the children normally have no opportunity except by accident of seeing their parents naked or witnessing the parts of an adult normally covered'.

The events which precipitated the High Court hearing

occurred after Annie had been taken into hospital for suspected pneumonia. Her parents had seemed attentive and loving, but as soon as she got to hospital the paediatrician in charge noticed that she began to withdraw from her parents and was very difficult with them. At first both he and the parents thought it was due to the unfamiliar surroundings and the antibiotic drugs administered to her. Then one night a nurse on a routine ward round began to take her pulse and the child woke up and started screaming, 'Daddy, don't do that. You know you aren't supposed to do that.' The nurse was very worried because she could not recall any other child screaming with so much terror when approached at night, however ill they appeared. So she reported the episode next day to the paediatrician in charge.

The paediatrician knew about the work of the Great Ormond Street unit and had attended seminars on their techniques. He thought there were grounds for suspecting that Annie had been sexually abused and he tried to arrange an interview for her with a psychiatric clinic as soon as he could. Unfortunately everything was booked up. So he decided the next best thing was to interview Annie himself, using the special dolls with adult sexual parts. He did his best to make the little girl relaxed, although from the start of the interview she was 'guarded and uncooperative'. He gradually introduced the dolls and got Annie to undress them. When she came to undress the male doll she became 'quite frozen when confronted with the doll's penis'. The reaction was so extreme that the paediatrician told the court that he could even now recall the electric effect. He thought her reaction very odd, as non-abused children are normally quite curious and most relaxed when they see the genital parts of the dolls. Somewhat concerned, the paediatrician decided that Annie should be seen by the experts at Great Ormond Street.

An interview was arranged, but the parents were not told why she was really attending. They were left with the impression that it was a further medical check-up. There were good reasons for this since Annie had remained dramatically withdrawn although she appeared to have recovered physically. So the parents were not in the least alarmed about the appointment. When they arrived at Great Ormond Street, they were themselves asked some very general questions about their family, then Annie was taken on her own to be interviewed by one of the team's most experienced social workers, Marianne Tranter. The paediatrician stayed with her throughout the interview, which was videotaped.

It became quite clear to the interviewer, during the course of the hour, that Annie had been abused. Not only could she describe what had happened but she could illustrate the events quite plainly on the dolls. She left them in no doubt that her mother had been aware of all this and had made no effort to prevent it.

They returned to the parents and told them what had happened and they were absolutely stupefied with horror, shock and disbelief. A medical examination followed which revealed nothing. The parents requested a second opinon. So another psychiatrist, who was not a specialist in child abuse, saw her and thought that although the child clearly had some 'particular difficulties' with her father, 'the nature of those difficulties was unclear'.

What then became central was whether the child was actually telling the truth or whether her interview was unreliable. The interview was indeed roundly attacked at the High Court hearing by the second, non-specialist psychiatrist, which fuelled the judge's misgivings. The judge was particularly concerned about the use of leading questions which are quite unacceptable in court, although as we have seen they might be quite appropriate in another context. Inevitably the judge could not divorce himself from his own legal traditions and he listed three types of questions 'which could only be to prompt the child's response'. First he objected to the use of leading questions. For example, the notion of ejaculation was introduced to the child's mind by the question 'When daddy does that, does it ever feel a bit wet down there?' Next the judge voiced disapproval of hypothetical questions, illustrated by 'What would you say if Dad tickles you there and you didn't like it?' 'I would say, Stop it, Daddy.' 'Would he always tickle you on the outside or would he sometimes tickle you on the inside?' 'In the inside.' The third style of questioning that the judge objected to was what he called cross-examination, which he said was 'exemplified by the following exchange: "Is there a private bit of Dad he would put there?" "No." "Does he sometimes put his willy there?" Nods head.'

All of those questions were thought to be 'suggestive' and it was thought unlikely that the child would have mentioned the acts featured in her answers had not the interviewer put them into her mind. The questions the judge approved of were those which he called 'neutral', where for example the child was asked 'What is happening now?' and she answered, 'I can feel a little bit of wet on the outside of my bottom.'

Both counsel for the defence and the rival psychiatrist joined in the attack on the interview methods. The rival psychiatrist was critical of the type of doll used. Defence counsel dismissed the overall method of interviewing, which he considered, not surprisingly, to be 'wholly inappropriate'. He thought it belonged to the realm of therapy, not to the field of diagnosis at all.

In the end the parents, although still denying abuse, agreed to accept treatment, and that allowed the judge to make a decision about the child. He concluded that there had 'been a degree of sexual interference by the father and that the mother was aware of this conduct and took no steps to prevent it'. Overall he thought that the interview on video 'was not an acceptable substitute for the overall view which the court has to take of the evidence as whole'. The child became a ward of court and both she and her sister were taken away from the parents and put into care, until some rehabilitation programme could be worked out.

At the end of the case, the conclusions of the Great Ormond Street unit prevailed, although their technique came in for a great deal of 'legal' criticism. But it is difficult to understand how any of this process is in the best interest of the child. During the course of her interview Annie had been asked, 'What does Daddy think would happen if you told someone else?' and she had answered, 'They would take me away. They would think he would have done something wrong when he hadn't.' She had added, 'I would like Mummy to tell him to stop doing it and go into his own bedroom.' Clearly Annie's worst fears were for her to be taken away for having told, and what she wanted was for the abuse to stop and her mother to support her. Instead of which a decision was made to take her away and to keep her mother and father together. Her worst fears had come true. For her own protection, she had been isolated and banished. The judge had rightly been concerned that the father might continue his abuse as he had not fully come to admit what he had done. But instead of removing the potential abuser, he removed the child. The judge not only had doubts about the way children were interviewed, he also had a fairly restricted view of the child's best interest in this case.

The decisions in the court are surprisingly inconsistent. Annie, a little five-year-old from a middle-class home, was put into care although her parents had agreed to treatment. The judge had accepted the child's testimony although unhappy about the interview. But in a case heard within two months of Annie's, where again the Great Ormond Street unit had interviewed the child, another judge severely criticized their methods, refused to accept the unit's conclusion from the interview, because it flagrantly disregarded the evidential requirements, and sent Marigold, a seven-year-old, back to her mother and her mother's boyfriend, who were both unemployed and known heroin addicts.

The case of Marigold was heard in the summer of 1986 in the High Court. Marigold had been temporarily put into a foster-home while her mother, who was known to take drugs, sorted out a few problems. During her stay she asked the foster-father several times to tickle the top of her leg, and then pulled his hand between her legs. The foster-parents became concerned and finally referred her to Great Ormond Street Hospital, where the child was interviewed for two hours on video. The team who conducted the interview found that it was one of the clearest cases of sexual abuse they had come across, and they were as certain as they could be that sexual abuse had taken place. In fact the accusations were quite severe. The interviewers thought that her mother's boyfriend had had vaginal, anal and oral intercourse with the child and had been masturbated by her. They were in no doubt about it, and left alone they would have begun some course of treatment for the child.

The judge, however, would have none of it. He found that 'it is unlikely that sexual abuse has taken place on the particular evidence of this particular case'. He sent the girl home 'forthwith'. His only concern was that the addicted parents should guarantee that they would stay clear of drugs. In this case, because this was a civil hearing in the Family Division of the High Court, Marigold did not have to go through the harrowing business of appearing at a criminal trial, facing the defendant. But it remains very doubtful whether Marigold's best interests were served.

Marigold had not had an easy life. She lived with her step-brother who was fourteen, her mother, who had been a heroin addict for some time, and her mother's current cohabitee, who was also a heroin addict. There had been a series of family crises and the social services had been involved with the family since Marigold had been one year old. The social workers were concerned about conditions in the home. Marigold had often been found unkempt, there appeared to be no discipline in the home, the children had often been late for school and there was what was politely described as 'a degree of chaos in the home'. When Marigold was six, her mother had deteriorated considerably and had been unable to cope. Marigold had been sent to a foster-home and her mother had gone to hospital for detoxification, which the judge found 'very much to her credit'.

The allegations concerned the mother's current boyfriend and Marigold. But both the mother and her boyfriend vehemently denied any acts of indecency. Marigold had displayed extremely precocious behaviour which was consistent with sexual abuse and had been sent to the Great Ormond Street clinic because of that suspicion. Not surprisingly she was more than a little reticent about what had gone on. Her answers and behaviour convinced the therapist but were not clear and spontaneous enough for the courtroom. A typical passage was as follows:

Q: It's a bit hard to talk about, isn't it? Would you ever ask him to stop if he put his willy into your bottom?

A: Yes.

Q: Yes. And would he stop or would he carry on? What did he used to do?

A: Don't know.

Q: Did Marigold used to feel quite upset sometimes and did she used to cry sometimes?

A: ... for Mummy.

Q: You cried for Mummy. You cried sometimes and what would happen to you if you cried for Mummy? Did Mummy come in [Brings out Mummy doll] I wonder if we can bring Mummy out. If you cried would Mummy come in then? Come on, let's have Mummy doll, and what would Mummy doll do now? What do you think?

A: Don't know.

Q: What will she say to Daddy?

A: Don't know. Stop.

Q: Stop, don't do that, and would he stop?

A: Yes.

It is difficult, without seeing the child react, to know whether she was surprised at these questions or understood them perfectly. Certainly an innocent seven-year-old would have been completely amazed at the questions. Marigold did not appear to be. But the judge dismissed this bit of evidence quite smartly, saying 'That is how the allegation in relation to the mother's participation came into the interview.'

The suggestion of oral intercourse was also not well received by the judge who commented: 'Marigold first indicated using the doll's neck, then the interviewer asked, "Did his willy sometimes get caught up a little bit above your neck [pointing to the mouth] a little bit?" Marigold then nodded. "Did it sometimes get a bit caught up in here in your mouth? Was that nice when he did that?" Marigold: "No."'

But what clearly concerned him the most, and where he began to show real irritation, was a passage that referred to masturbation. In this he was supported by a rival child psychiatrist. Marigold was asked to show the interviewer how she would touch her mother's boyfriend's penis. The interviewer offered her finger for Marigold to demonstrate. Marigold giggled and touched the finger quickly. There then ensued among these eminent men in the courtroom a discussion about whether that did or did not in fact constitute knowledge of masturbation. The rival psychiatrist apparently 'did not think that the gesture made by Marigold was a masturbatory gesture'. The judge added, 'I am bound to say my impression was that the movement made by Marigold with her finger would not normally be described as a masturbatory gesture.'

Overall the judge was inclined to side with one of the rival
psychiatrists who was 'horrified' at the techniques used.
Throughout the interview there had been an assumption of
abuse, he claimed, so even if the child denied it, the interviewer
bulldozed on with her questions assuming she had not denied
it. Typically they ran: 'Did he ever ask you to touch him?' 'No.'
'If he had asked you to touch him how would he have liked you
to do it?' The rival psychiatrist believed 'It should be unethical
to use this technique as an exploratory technique in the case
of non-admitted child abuse.' It had not been a spontaneous
interview. The child had not been allowed to prattle away freely.
She had answered the questions that were in the interviewer's
mind. The interviewer had led the witness and suggested
answers.

The interview methods became central to the case. The fact
that the child had clearly displayed some very strange behavioural traits with her foster-parents was discounted. The evidence
of the therapist who had interviewed her was also discounted.
An expert in these matters, the therapist has been interviewing
at Great Ormond Street for the last five years specifically about
sexual abuse. In her evidence she pointed out that Marigold had
a degree of sexual knowledge which is unusual in a child of her
age. She felt that the risk of the child being abused in the future
if she returned home was high. She concluded by saying that it
was one of the clearest cases of sexual abuse which she had
come across.

There is no doubt that pressure was brought on the child to
admit what had happened. The therapist felt that that was
necessary to help the child talk and overcome the trauma which
she had suffered. The judge in his summing-up commented:

> The object is to get children to talk about what has happened
> and that is of course very plaudible [sic]. However, there
> must undoubtedly in using that technique be a very real risk
> that the child will say that something has occurred which
> has not. It is common ground that the technique is to some
> extent still in its experimental stages and at the moment I
> must have some reservations as to whether the technique
> used in interviewing the children does necessarily elicit the
> truth.

The judge decided that Marigold should be sent back to her home as soon as possible, providing that her mother and co-habitee could be shown to be drug-free.

Clearly these interviews, although they touch on a number of problems, are useless as evidence because of the leading questions. Yet they are being dragged into the courts and dissected by professionals who have expertise in the law rather than in therapy. Recently Dr Vizard addressed the argument in public:

> Who is to interpret the visual record of a therapist's interview? Is it to be the highly trained legal experts in court, who are, nevertheless, lay persons with respect to psychiatry? Is it to be the therapist who conducted the interview or is it to be a second or third expert, called in to give an opinion on the visual record, perhaps not seeing the child at all? Is there any onus on the agency requesting the second or third opinion or on the courts to ensure that these experts are trained specifically in child-abuse work?

The problem, as she recognizes only too well, lies in the interviewing techniques: 'Experienced officers will agree that some degree of "leading" a child may be necessary to help the child talk, whilst we are all agreed that this very process undermines the evidential value of what is then disclosed.... Is there any way out of this dilemma?'

Mr Justice Latey, addressing the same problem in May 1986, commented: 'I am simply not equipped to suggest whether a modification of the technique could be made so as better to meet the forensic need without seriously undermining the therapeutic need. It may not be possible. Or it may be possible. As I see it, it is for the clinical experts to explore this and perhaps experiment.'

The clinical experts are very busy exploring it, to try and find a way of making their interviews fit in with legal requirements. After a spate of bad publicity, Dr Bentovim decided to have two-part interviews, one where the questions were open and as neutral as possible, and one where questions were leading. The real issue is whether their methods should have to change because of legal requirements. If they find that their methods do not work for their own treatment, presumably they will change. But should they have to meet the requirements of a court?

If the High Court and the juvenile courts demand to see videos, to establish factual events that are legally acceptable, interviews should be carried out by professionals who are skilled in legal or criminal investigation. Scotland Yard have in fact just pioneered a new experiment which trains police and social services to do joint interviews. None of the videos they have made so far have reached the courts, because they are still not admissible in criminal cases. But they could well provide a blueprint for statements in civil proceedings. Detective Superintendent Peter Gwynne of Scotland Yard, who started the project, described his aims to us: 'What I want is an evidentially sound video, one that judges will accept, that doesn't have leading questions. They will not be like those taken for clinical material. Police officers are skilled in investigation and asking questions. They're fully aware of the rules of evidence and admissibility. What we've tried to do is give the social workers those skills and the interview will be one the courts will readily accept as being a true record of what took place and there's no criticism about it.'

There should be room for both types of interview: one that satisfies the court and one that gives the child some therapeutic relief. It is unlikely that the investigative one will in all cases reveal the abuse. A certain amount of leading questioning and suggestion does often seem to be necessary.

Current research shows that children are fundamentally truthful even if they are asked leading and suggestive questions. Children appear remarkably truthful when they report events they were involved in, and quite accurate. The younger they are the more likely they are to forget more things over time, but they are no more suggestible than adults.

In the last few years, research psychologists in America have developed convincing experiments which test how truthfully children remember events. One of the most original of these psychologists is Gail Goodman, Professor of Psychology at the University of Denver. Her fascination with child witnesses has grown as she has repeatedly discovered, contrary to what most adults believe, that children tend to recall accurately an event that they witnessed or took part in. They often forget incidental details like the picture on the wall, the colour of a jacket, the exact time of day, failure which can be extremely trying if they are called upon to give evidence. But they do not lie and are no more open to suggestion than adults.

To test how difficult it is to influence witnesses and make them describe events that had not occurred, Professor Goodman and her researcher Leslie Rudy constructed an experiment that has been refined over the years. They arranged for pairs of children aged four and seven to go into a caravan where they met a researcher. One of the children was selected to play with the researcher, the other was told to watch. The researcher then dressed up the child, made up his or her face and took photographs. He then picked him or her up, and played a few games, making sure he called the child by name. The other child just passively watched. All of this was videoed. Eleven days later both children were questioned about what went on. A large number of the questions were leading – for example, 'He took your clothes off, didn't he? What did he put in your mouth? How many times did he hit you?' All the seven-year-olds answered truthfully, 'No, he didn't take off my clothes,' etc. and made no errors at all. Even the four-year-olds made very few errors.

There were absolutely no false reports of abuse at all, despite the fact that some of the interviewing techniques were designed to suggest this very persuasively. If anything there were omissions, rather than admissions of false events. Some of the children said 'He did not touch me,' or 'He did not touch me on the mouth,' when it was obvious from the video that the child *had* been touched.

There was a very small percentage (2 per cent) of the very youngest, three to four years old, who claimed that they had been kissed, when clearly they had not. Interestingly, when they were pressed for details they could not describe any, although their memory was quite clear on other events.

Encouraged by these results Goodman and her team wanted to see how children might react once they had been abused. Obviously they could not research on real abuse, but, to simulate it as closely as possible, they decided to observe an event where the children might be frightened or even traumatized and find out how accurately they could describe that experience.

Goodman devised a brilliant scenario. She got permission from a clinic to video pre-school children (aged five and six) receiving their inoculations. They paid the families for taking part and recorded the experiences of a group of children. Some of the children were terrified and screamed, some were withdrawn, others were not at all affected.

The children were brought back after four days and after nine days and were questioned on what had happened. Some of the questions were deliberately leading. They were asked, for example, 'Did they kiss you? Did they hit you? Were you touched anywhere besides your arm? Had you seen this person before?'

Goodman's team found that, whether the children had been frightened or not, they remembered the events clearly and accurately. They could not elaborate in any detail about the objects in the room, or the precise colour of the doctor's hair, but they did not distort anything that was central to the event. They found the younger ones more suggestible and relatively easy to influence about the peripheral issues – on the nurse's appearance, the colour of the room, whether someone wore spectacles. But they were very difficult to influence about what anyone had actually done to them. Goodman concluded that the children were far less open to suggestion than anyone had thought.

The children were all asked whether they knew the difference between truth and lies, to see whether that ability had an effect on what they remembered. It is assumed, particularly in courtrooms, that if children can distinguish between truth and falsehood their testimony will be more reliable. In the Goodman study, the ability to understand the difference between truth and lies had no perceptible effect on whether the children remembered the basic events accurately. Curiously, however, it did predict the way they could be influenced, but not in the way anyone had expected. The children who were conceptually able to understand the meaning of truth turned out to be more easily open to suggestion than those who could not conceptually understand the difference between truth and falsehood.

One year after the experiment, Goodman decided to test the children's memory once more. Instead of putting the questions yet again she decided to set the whole project into a legal context.

A case was devised which concerned damages for negligence. The child was to be the chief witness in the case. The prosecution alleged that negligence had occurred because the doctor had wrongfully administered a vaccination. The doctor, and defence, were claiming that no vaccination had taken place.

Two attorneys were employed, one for the defence, one for the prosecution, and each of the children was cross-examined as if in a witness box. They were asked details of the event. The defence put it to them that perhaps they had not actually received the vaccination, and questioned their accuracy and memory on other minor details in the room.

Six children were cross-examined in this way and became the chief and only witnesses for six different juries, who were matched as far as possible with a real jury. The jury were asked how accurate they thought the child was about the individuals in the room, about the doctor, about the location and about the time. The child had also been asked to identify someone on a photo line-up, and the jury were asked whether they could believe the child. At the end of the experiment the jury had to decide who was guilty. Only one person could be telling the truth: was it the doctor or the child? The researchers, of course, knew the answer, as they had recorded the original event. The mock juries were not told about that.

The results showed that the adult juries tended not to believe the children. Even the children who were very accurate tended not to be believed. When asked at what age children might have more credibility they consistently said twelve to fourteen. They felt that the young children they had seen testify were very easily manipulated by their legal counsel. Juries thought only the older children would be able to withstand that pressure.

The children had in fact been truthful. Many of the details had been forgotten over time, but they remembered the key events well. Despite the fact that defence counsel tried to confuse them and undermine their credibility, they remained remarkably consistent. They did not fabricate any event that had not taken place. Nonetheless, they were not believed.

The conclusion is stark. The real problem is not whether children tell the truth, but whether adults are prepared to believe them. It seems that it is the adults' view of children which needs attention. And this must apply particularly to the legal

profession with its passion for testing whether or not children
know the difference between truth and lies. In Britain, if children
cannot differentiate conceptually between truth and falsehood,
they remain unsworn and their testimony unreliable. Yet the
evidence in Goodman's study shows that this particular intellectual abstraction made no difference. Those who understood
the difference between truth and falsehood were as accurate as
those who did not understand.

Useful lessons could no doubt be learned from all this by legal
counsel. Children will forget minor details. Children can get
confused by dates and times. Children will often omit important
details. But it would be tragic if others did not also learn that
children remembered faithfully core events, those that they
experienced and those that they witnessed.

To guarantee the child a proper hearing the West Germans
appoint a psychologist in every case of alleged child sexual
abuse. The Germans do not have an adversarial system of
criminal justice like that in Britain and the USA. They have an
inquisitorial system which is primarily concerned with gathering
all the possible evidence in a case, instead of the adversarial
marshalling of a case for the prosecution and a case for the
defence. In the pre-trial phase, before a case ever gets to court,
a psychological expert will be commissioned to decide whether
or not the child is telling the truth. The expert will then help
the prosecution to decide whether or not there is a case to
answer. If someone is charged, the psychological expert will
continue with the case and will appear for both prosecution and
defence as an 'aid to the court'. Specifically he will be used to
evaluate certain evidence and judge the witness's credibility.

The idea that a psychological expert could ascertain the
credibility of a witness which in turn could lead to a formal
indictment is light years away from the charming British muddle
we described earlier in the chapter. It would be even more
difficult for most of the courts in Britain to grasp that the experts
who work in the German courts have a clear, logical nineteen-
point system to test the children which is based on research and
is administered with uniform care. The children's verbal and
reasoning skills are established by inviting them to describe in
detail a familiar event. The assumption throughout is that a
fabricated story is different from a real experience: it tends

to be more logical, has less detail, is less eccentric and more stereotyped. By contrast, children telling the truth tend to be more self-critical and contradictory, admit to being forgetful and so on. The nineteen-point scale, which is weighted, plays an important role in the evidence. Sometimes the psychologist is challenged and cross-examined. But the expert method remains one that professionals working with the children and in the law accept and recognize as valid.

There is enough evidence and research into children's truthfulness and memory to develop a systematic approach to children's tales of sexual abuse. If we are, as we continue to claim, acting 'in the best interests of the child', then surely this must be a priority.

# 7   THE PSYCHOLOGICAL TIME BOMB

All the evidence suggests that child sexual abuse is of epidemic proportions and that what we are seeing is only the tip of the iceberg. As soon as it is made possible for people to seek help, and some promise of support is made public, there seems to be no end to the demand. When the model Child Assault Treatment programme in Santa Clara County, California, was developed and publicized in 1969 there was a 3,000 per cent increase in reported cases over seven years. Whereas the rate elsewhere in the USA averages 1·4 per thousand, in Santa Clara it is three times that. So it looks as if the real incidence rates are far higher than figures suggest. The recent launch, in October 1986, of BBC Television's Child Line was another example. The organizers were quite unprepared for the scale of the response: they had thousands of serious and desperate calls. Within weeks they had completely to reorganize.

Dr Tony Baker, a psychiatrist at Queen Mary's Hospital for children, and Dr Sylvia Duncan, a clinical psychologist at Charing Cross Hospital, commissioned a national sample in Britain and found that 10 per cent of men and women over sixteen reported that they had been sexually abused before the age of sixteen. Half the abusers were known to their victims. Baker and Duncan concluded that these figures underestimate the problem and inferred:

> Taking what must then be a conservative estimate of a 10 per cent prevalence of child sexual abuse in Great Britain, we can begin to estimate the size of the problem. A possible

4.5 million adults (fifteen years and over) will have been sexually abused as children and a potential 1,117,000 children in the general population will be sexually abused by the age of fifteen years. An estimated 143,000 of these will be abused within the family.

Social services departments are groaning under the sudden influx of new suspected sexual-abuse cases. Most have no expertise in this field and are severely stretched dealing with all the other forms of child abuse. To add to the complications there are no definitive procedures in Britain. The DHSS has draft guidelines which insist that the welfare of the child must be the overriding concern, and counsels against repeated medical examinations. Above all it emphasizes the importance of co-operation between police, social workers and doctors.

The most recent survey (by P. Mrazek) in Britain of victims seen by professionals, including police surgeons, paediatricians, GPs and child psychiatrists, makes depressing reading. There is a noticeable lack of collaboration between the various professionals and agencies and there are no elaborate checking procedures like the area review committees that have sprung up to deal with physical abuse. Nearly half the cases were prosecuted but very few of the victims received any social-work or therapeutic help. The only form of protection and help for the child had been the prosecution and imprisonment of the offender.

The present emphasis on the law in sexual abuse will come as no surprise to anyone who has studied the history of child abuse. Dr Henry Kempe, the pioneer researcher into child abuse, has outlined six stages of awareness that communities have gone through. First, there is a denial that abuse is significant or widespread. It is seen as aberrant and due to psychotic, drunken or drugged parents, nothing to do with the community. Second, people begin to take note of the more lurid and brutal forms of abuse – the battered child – and to find ways of dealing with it as a social problem by intervening and recognizing less severe abuse earlier. Third, attention moves on to more subtle abuse, such as neglect and failure to thrive. Fourth, there is a recognition of emotional neglect and abuse, and concern about the effects of rejection and scapegoating. Fifth, there is a slow,

painful recognition of the existence of sexual abuse. To begin
with, it was considered to be a series of isolated events. Gradually, echoing the reaction to physical abuse, those working with
children realized how widespread the problem was – yet no one
quite knew how to deal with it. Today's reaction to the problem
of sexual abuse bears a striking resemblance to the way 'the
battered-baby syndrome' was received some fifteen to twenty
years ago. Finally, at the sixth stage there is a belief and
guarantee that every child is wanted and receives proper food,
health care and loving attention.

One of the reasons why the professionals learned to hammer
out a joint approach on battered children was a series of very
public, very sensational inquiries into the killings of certain
children. This forced those looking after children to work out
how and why it happened, and how it could be prevented and
treated. Even then it took some time before the various agencies,
police, social services, doctors and health services worked out
guidelines and procedures. And as we have seen in earlier chap-
ters there is still some way to go.

Sexual abuse, although potentially damaging, is not lethal, so
there is less initial public outrage. But because it is so secret,
and because even talking about a taboo subject is taboo, there
is a conspiracy of silence about the problem. This in turn means
that there is no consistent approach, no accepted treatment,
no common understanding. Each local authority and police
department is left to deal with it as they see fit. In areas where
the problem is tackled seriously, that response appears to be
due to a few imaginative individuals. Most of the rest flounder
in a persistent and inaccurate mythology aggravated by lack of
training and shortage of staff.

We recently attended a packed public meeting on child sexual
abuse held primarily for doctors and medical students. One of
the panel described how difficult it was to handle the children
who talk about someone abusing them. She told a sad tale about
a twelve-year-old girl who had had some difficulties at school.
Finally after a long talk with her teacher the girl had blurted
out that her father had been molesting her for some time. The
teacher was very sympathetic, and said perhaps she should go
home and think about what she had said before taking it any
further. The girl, very upset, went home and, as would be

expected, told her father about the conversation at school. The father was angry and threatened the girl; the next day she returned to school and retracted the entire story. This particular example was used to show not simply that people must be prepared to believe a child, but that they have to learn to listen and hear. That presupposes that there is a willingness to listen and some general understanding of sexual assault.

At the same meeting, the audience grew gradually restless after an hour of experts talking in general about the theory of sexual abuse and the law. Then they were shown a video of a child describing in graphic detail extraordinary sexual acts that his father had made him perform. The atmosphere became electric. The audience were clearly shocked and stunned. They all wanted to know what to do if they were faced with a similar case. The panel was unsure, but after some hesitation they suggested that the best course would be to inform the social services. But few social services departments are equipped to deal with these problems yet. Even more than physical abuse, sexual abuse is a problem that requires very special knowledge and special skills. It requires co-ordinated treatment and a multi-disciplinary approach. It will not be enough to dump this problem too on social workers who have no special training.

It had proved difficult, as Kempe predicted, to make those working in the field address sexual abuse in a clinical way. Psychiatrists, doctors and researchers working in this area continuously come up against the disbelief and hostility of their colleagues. While most professionals and the public can understand occasional or persistent outbreaks of violence, it is quite repulsive to think of an adult in a protective role forcing a small child into advanced sexual games. It also arouses all types of personal sexual feelings which may attract and incite, horrify or numb those involved. It is easier then not to see and not to hear. S.M. Sgroi, a pioneering American doctor in this field, wrote: 'Recognition of sexual molestation of a child is entirely dependent on the individual's inherent willingness to entertain the possibility that the condition may exist.'

In Texas the social services department told us that the only way they could convince the public that there was a problem and that the statistics meant something was to show videos of the children talking about what had happened to them. That made people face the issue and accept the need for changes in the law and for a large specialist treatment programme. If sexual abuse thrives on secrecy, every aspect of the issue should be made as public as possible.

By far the most important reason for facing up to the problem is its long-term effects. Sexual assault has been called a 'psychological time bomb' which can seriously affect a child's development. Many eminent professionals would agree with Freud's original diagnosis that it is the major cause of neurosis. Breaking tradition with her illustrious father Anna Freud was moved to write in 1981: 'Where the chances of harming a child's normal development are concerned, incest ranks higher than abandonment, neglect, physical maltreatment or any other form of abuse. It would be a total mistake to underrate the implications or frequency of its actual occurrence.'

Many paediatricians, psychologists and criminologists would go much further and claim that running away, adolescent drug addiction and prostitution, somatic complaints, sexual deviance, marital problems, suicidal tendencies and hysterical seizures could all be associated with sexual assault. Short- and long-term effects are now well documented. In 1984 Dr Kempe, who ran a large centre for abused children in Denver, Colorado, wrote:

> Let me add that those who believe incest best left a family affair, that it is not of serious emotional import as judged by the fact that many victims have gone on to lead apparently normal lives ... fail to take into account the enormous emotional costs paid by many of these children and the scars they bear for a lifetime. Recent studies have shown that a disproportionate number of prostitutes have been involved in incest in early years and that most children involved in incest do not grow up to have happy lives.

David Finkelhor, one of the most internationally respected specialists working in this field, concluded, after a survey in 1986 of the research to date, 'As evidence now accumulates it conveys a clear suggestion that sexual abuse is a serious mental health problem consistently associated with very disturbing subsequent problems in a significant proportion of its victims.' The most telling research shows that a great number of yesterday's victims are tomorrow's perpetrators. An eminent psychiatrist, John Hamilton, has analysed the 'interplay between offender and victim' and found that a high proportion of offenders had themselves been victims. Mothers who murdered had been battered. Men who had been sexually abused became abusers. Above all those who had been dominated, humiliated and coerced by the needs and demands of their parents, whether emotional, physical or sexual, would be likely to turn to psychopathic behaviour as adults.

Case-histories continue to reveal that pattern. We saw one interview on video that illustrates this vicious cycle. A small boy recounted in a fairly matter-of-fact way a routine of sexual acts that he had had to perform with his father. Many of them were fairly brutal, and certainly the boy did not seem to have any choice in the matter. His father was a headmaster, used to giving orders and being obeyed. The boy explained, without emotion, 'My dad said his dad had done it to him, and when I grew up I would do the same thing to my son. So I just thought it was part of life.'

Girls are no less at risk and when they are adults often display what G. Berry, an American psychiatrist, has so dramatically called the 'incest carrier syndrome'. These 'carriers' have no idea how to protect their own daughters and continuously associate with men who are child molesters. So the hapless daughters of women who have been assaulted tend in some remorseless way to become victims themselves.

The most comprehensive English study compiled by a group of eminent lawyers, psychiatrists, paediatricians, police and social workers (the CIBA Foundation), *Child Sexual Abuse within the Family*, commented:

Adults who have been sexually abused in childhood have a poor sense of their own worth; they are often depressed; they describe a sense of pollution, contamination, and dirtiness. Frequently the victims feel abandoned by their mothers and recreate essentially abusive relationships in their search for a cure. Sexually abused parents often abuse sexually and physically their own children. They experience physical affection towards their infants not as nurturing but as having a sexual meaning. They combine severe physical

punishment with for example kisses on the child's mouth
and stroking of their genitals, a repetition of their own
experiences. The evidence so far suggests that sexual abuse
may have lasting adverse consequences in adult life,
especially on sexuality and the ability to bring up children.

Once recognized and treated, there is a chance that the next
generation will avoid some of this pain and destruction. But to
break the vicious generational cycle, experts believe that we
have to go beyond the simple prosecution of perpetrators and
plan some general prevention and treatment. Victims need help
to make them aware of what has happened and try to stop them
damaging themselves and the next generation. Often that can
only happen in the context of their families. So the family too
need help to deal with their dreadful wounds. Finally there has
to be a slightly less jaundiced view of offenders. Those who go
to prison will eventually come out again. Not all of them are
incurable. If they are given no support they are likely to reoffend.
All the evidence from Britain and the USA shows that child
molesters have a very high rate of recidivism.

It is only in the 1980s that there has been any attempt to deal
with sexual abuse as a serious social and psychological problem.
The British approach is still patchy and uncoordinated.

The procedures are hopelessly vague. We were researching in
a social services department when a nursery teacher phoned to
report a child whose vagina looked unnaturally swollen. The
social workers were caught unawares. They spent a long time
trying to work out whether the child should be seen by the local
doctor or the police doctor or should be taken to the hospital.
They eventually took her to a local doctor whose report was equi-
vocal. Then there was a dilemma about what to do next. They
called the local police, but then decided it would be best if someone interviewed the child before the perpetrator, the father,
was approached. So they tried to find some psychiatrist to do a
'disclosure interview' on video. But the three units they tried
were all booked up for weeks and could not see them. They
were not sure whether to talk to the child, whether to keep the
child away from the mother, whether to let the police take over.
They had nowhere to turn to for advice.

There are areas where the police and social services have hammered out a joint approach to avoid this type of confusion and panic. Northamptonshire, Cardiff, Devon, Hampshire, Newcastle and Northumbria and Bexley all publicize their methods of joint initial interviews by both police and social services that allow the social workers to look after the child and the police to worry about the criminal procedures. In those areas police and social services have begun to understand that there has to be special knowledge. Devon has appointed child-abuse liaison officers who specialize in this area alone and are trained to untangle the complex emotions and obligations that are set in motion once an allegation has been made. They consult with all the possible agencies before prosecuting, in order to avoid the family tragedy of a wrongful arrest. Alternatively, they move in swiftly on more certain cases to avoid retractions or repeat offences. They tend to caution in a large number of first cases instead of prosecuting. This is by no means standard procedure. In other authorities, if there happens to be an enlightened inspector (like Trevor Buckroyd in Leeds) some expertise will be brought to the case, but that is a matter of luck rather than thoughtful planning.

Treatment is even more haphazard. A great deal of lip-service is paid to the trauma a child suffers if the father is suddenly taken away and to the guilt he or she feels for breaking up the family, but arrangements to ease this are practically non-existent. Incest Crisis Line operates on a voluntary basis in Britain but it has only a few telephone lines and they are almost permanently engaged. There are various self-help groups for parents dotted about the country, the odd survivor group and support groups for mothers. There is a minimal amount of therapy, some organized through the probation service, and some hospital-based as at Great Ormond Street. The NSPCC has pioneered groups for victims and offenders in places like Cardiff, Rochdale and Manchester. But the pattern is random and bewildering. In Britain the problem is so new that the DHSS is only just about to set up a working party to look into training. Social workers, who are in the front line of referrals, have no particular expertise in this area. We have seen the difficulties that are caused by lack of specialist knowledge in other fields of abuse. Sexual abuse is if anything more complicated and calls for similar specialist skills.

Sexual abuse cannot be viewed simply as a criminal offence since its ramifications for the family and victim are well documented. Like physical abuse, it is an everyday problem which to the trained eye has fairly consistent features. There is now a great deal of empirical evidence and research about how, where and why it occurs. Most of it is hidden away in learned journals and professional manuals. The grim facts that emerge contradict simple popular stereotypes.

It certainly bears no relation to the ordinary notions of sexual activity, which assume something loving, tender, exciting and reciprocal. Children experience none of this. They are ordered to do certain acts, trained to continue them and terrorized into submission. Almost all children report being frightened. One boy we learned about had to mop up the blood dribbling down his leg after his father had finished with him, and was hit around the head if he stopped masturbating his father too soon. There was not much affection or reciprocity there. In some cases a child may seem to be a willing partner and get some physical satisfaction but it is still impossible for that child to give proper consent. The child cannot make an informed decision, because it has no information on which to base it. A child has no power to say no to a controlling adult and no way of knowing whether what he is doing is really wrong. Here the sexual act is a violation, not a sign of affection. As Kempe wrote in 1978: 'Sexual abuse is defined as the involvement of dependent, developmentally immature children and adolescents in sexual activities they do not truly comprehend, to which they are unable to give informed consent, or that violate the social taboos of family roles.'

There is also a widely held notion that those who are involved are nubile adolescents. Pubescent pin-ups appear in glossy magazines pouting provocatively. They have become an acceptable part of male, and possibly female, sexual fantasy. But the victims are not the Lolitas. In fact, girls over thirteen are almost immune from incestuous relationships, unless they continue ones that have begun earlier. The average girl victim is under ten when she begins, and may be as young as two or three. In all the surveys girls as young as nine months have been badly assaulted.

It is a chilling thought and one which is very difficult to accept. The full horror only dawned on us when we met a little four-year-old, whose father had assaulted her. She was dressed in her maroon school tunic, her hair done in two little bunches tied with ribbons. She sang nursery rhymes to herself and played on the floor with her dolls. It was quite sickening even to think of what might have happened to this fragile little child.

The most prevalent misconception, according to a recent research study in Boston by David Finkelhor, is that offenders are mostly strangers. Nothing could be further from the truth. Every study shows that strangers account for a small minority of child sexual abuse. Most studies report that only 25 per cent of the offenders were strangers, some report less. But warning girls to beware of strangers leaves them totally unprepared for the three-to-one chance that she will be approached by someone she has learned to obey and trust.

There do seem to be children who are considerably more at risk. Finkelhor's study found that the strongest risk factor was having a stepfather. It actually doubled the girl's risk of being abused. A stepfather was five times more likely to molest a daughter than the natural father. As if those figures were not dramatic enough, it appears that stepdaughters are not only more vulnerable at the hands of stepfathers but also seem to be more victimized by other men: they are five times more likely to become the victim of a friend of their parents.

This appears to be partly due to the child's relationship to her stepfather. If the father is traditional and holds very conservative attitudes towards obedience, authority and the sub-ordination of women, the daughter seems to be more at risk. If he is not very affectionate or very physical, she is at still greater risk. According to Finkelhor, if she is starved of affection from a father she is likely to search for it fairly indiscriminately elsewhere. If in addition she had been taught to obey adults without demur, she is likely to be even more vulnerable.

But another reason why girls are at risk arises out of their relationship, or lack of relationship, with their mothers. Girls who have not lived with their mothers for some time seem to be three times more vulnerable than other girls. It is not simply the physical absence of mothers – girls whose mothers go out to work are not considered more at risk. It is girls who have an extremely poor relationship with their mothers, who feel they are cold, distant or psychologically absent who are more consistently at risk.

Finkelhor's study showed quite clearly that where the mother is very dominated by her husband, where she is less well educated than her husband, her daughter is considerably more at risk. It is not dangerous for a girl to have parents who were both poorly educated, but there is a considerable risk if there is a distinct educational imbalance and the father is better educated and wields greater power and authority in the relationship.

Mothers who are strict and punitive, particularly about sexual matters, also seem to make their daughters more vulnerable. Mothers who criticize their daughters for asking sexual questions, and punish them for touching themselves or looking at sexual pictures, are more likely to have daughters who are abused. In fact, according to this same study, punitive mothers were the second most important risk factor after stepfathers. The girls who reported having mothers who were strict about these issues were 75 per cent more at risk than the 'typical' girl in the sample.

On the basis of this evidence the study produced a high-risk checklist containing eight conditions. These were:

– stepfather
– have lived without mother
– not close to mother
– mother never finished secondary school
– sex-punitive mother
– no physical affection from father
– income under $10,000 (£6,000)
– two friends or less in childhood

If girls have none of these conditions their risk is absolutely nil. As each condition is added, the risk factor increases by 15–20 per cent. Among those with five factors, two-thirds had been victimized. Those with all the conditions were at the greatest risk. This could well alert the professionals to the types of background which put certain children at risk.

The checklist of the 'lethal family' included poverty, economic stress and social isolation, features which could well tip the balance towards violence. But sexual abuse does not seem subject to the vagaries of class and money, although income is one item on the checklist. It knows no social boundaries. A doctor or barrister is as likely to assault his daughter as a coalminer or out-of-work labourer. A social worker in one area we visited refused to believe that the daughter of a barrister had been molested by her father. The child had been referred to the hospital with a bad case of cystitis. The child hinted at what had happened but both parents denied it. The social worker avoided the case, feeling much too troubled by its implications. She was finally relieved of it and it was given to a colleague. In due course the barrister was charged and given a suspended sentence.

Isolating the characteristics of high-risk children does not mean they can be identified, but it does show that the parents' own relationships to each other and to the child are central. That in itself causes extra pressures. If the relationships are cold or punitive, either prior to or because of the abuse, the child has no one to turn to, no one to confide in. The web of incest traps the child into indefinite silence. The real social problem is not that children tell lies, but that most never tell at all.

An American psychiatrist, Roland Summit, vividly outlines the child's dilemma in a process which he calls the 'accommodation syndrome'. Child victims pass through five stages: secrecy, helplessness, entrapment and accommodation, delayed disclosure and retraction.

*Secrecy.* Most children do not tell anyone after they have been assaulted, because they have been told to keep it a secret. This means above all not telling their mothers. So even if they do not quite understand what they have done, they have a strong sense that it is bad and wrong and that if they do tell they will be punished.

*Helplessness.* Even if the adult does not use force, it is difficult for a child to protect himself or herself, particularly against an adult in authority. The initial approaches are tentative, and only gradually become more advanced. The child is perfectly aware that the furtive approaches are not the normal displays of affection and feels increasingly guilty, isolated and helpless. More and more confused, the child is unable to fight off the approaches and passively accepts what happens. Even if a brother or sister is in the same room, the child is unlikely to call out for help. Summit explains: 'The natural ability to cry out or protect herself provides the core of misunderstanding between the victim and the community of adults as well as the breeding place for the child's later self-reprisals. Almost no adult seems willing to believe that a legitimate victim would remain still. She is expected to react with kicks and screams.'

*Entrapment and accommodation.* The child is told by the parent that being good means being submissive to his sexual demands. There are additional pressures, for if he or she is 'good' and keeps the secret he or she will not upset the mother, will prevent the father from moving on and molesting another daughter, and will make sure the father does not go to jail or get sent away. So the child is made to be ultimately responsible for keeping the family together. Good means keeping the secret, not telling the truth and holding the family together. In a bizarre reversal of morality, good means living a lie. Summit concludes: 'There is the inevitable splitting of moral values; maintaining a lie to keep the secret is the ultimate virtue, while telling the truth would be the greatest sin. A child thus victimized will appear to accept or seek sexual contact without complaint.' The child has complied, and has apparently accommodated the adult's perverse demands. But psychologically the cost is enormous. Inside he or she feels outrage at the violation and intense anger at having to tolerate this passive helplessness. But being a dependent child, it is impossible to turn that anger on to the parents, as he or she needs them to survive. So the child may express it actively against himself or herself by attempting suicide, running away, self-mutilation, promiscuity. Alternatively he or she may turn the hatred on the mother and blame her for not protecting him or her. This too has a terrible cost, for if a daughter cannot turn to her mother for support, she will continually seek out another assaulting male in the vain hope of getting some protection.

*Delayed disclosure.* Most assault is kept secret until adolescence. Then (like Donna) the victim will feel more able to stand up for herself and that in turn will make the father more jealous and controlling. Often there is a fight – about coming home late, going out with a boy, drinking, running away – and the father punishes the girl. At last she decides to tell all. But when she finally blurts out her story it is received with a degree of scepticism. After all, a rebellious teenager who claims to have been a victim for many years and to have remained silent has little credibility. Adults are likely to identify with the parent rather than the adolescent. An alternative accommodation for the child would be to become excessively conformist, striving to do well, and eager to please. If and when these children tell, they are even less likely to be believed. No one who appears outwardly so well adjusted could possibly be a cause for concern.

*Retraction.* It is very likely that a child who has told about incest will later deny it. The mother, who contrary to popular belief does not generally know what is going on, may then turn on the child. The father denies everything. The child sees all his or her worst fears about being responsible for breaking up the family coming true and finds it easier to return to his or her schizophrenic adaptation where 'good' means telling lies or keeping silent. Summit rounds off his model: 'This simple lie carries more credibility than the most explicit claims of incestuous entrapment. It confirms adult expectations that children cannot be trusted. It restores the precarious equilibrium of the family. The children learn not to complain. The adults learn not to listen. And the authorities learn not to believe rebellious children who try to use their sexual power to destroy well-meaning parents. Case closed.'

This sequence of events is particularly relevant to girls. Paula, who wrote to us when we began this research, recounted a personal history that uncannily mirrored this 'syndrome' and its effects. We visited her in her immaculate, neatly furnished post-war terraced house in south London. She had said she was willing to share her experiences with us, as she felt it was important that people should know about these things. She had only ever told her husband about what had happened. She had never mentioned it to anyone else in her family, not even to her sister. But she was willing to talk to a complete stranger.

Paula is forty-eight, married with two daughters aged seventeen and twenty. Her husband runs an office, and she has had a number of short-term jobs – currently she is hoping to work in a play-group. Plump, with an open, humorous face, she was very nervous when we met, and had written pages of notes to remind herself. Without any formalities she began: 'I always remember my grandfather touching me from the earliest days and I knew I didn't like it. I remember saying to my mother, "I don't like grandad tickling me," and my mother used to say, "Don't be silly." Whenever we were alone he would touch my legs and my breasts and then one day he went out and bought lots of cakes and sweets. He started to touch me a bit more, and then down there, and he used to give me cakes and sweets.

'That became a regular pattern of behaviour: he gave me sweets and then touched me. He used to buy me sweets regularly on Friday nights when my mother went out to do the family shopping because he was alone with me then. If I started to pull away or anything he would say, "Be still and just eat your cake." And then he got to the point when he was just kissing my vagina and as soon as my mother went out he would say, "Pull your knickers down," and he would begin. I knew it was wrong but I obeyed. I mean in those days you didn't disobey grown-ups.'

Paula could not remember how old she had been when all that had started. She thought she might have been about seven or eight. They progressed to intercourse by the time she was eleven or twelve. From then until she ran away from home at sixteen, he had intercourse with her regularly.

The way she adapted to her grandfather and to the confusion and isolation conforms exactly to the 'accommodation syndrome'. Describing her feelings Paula commented: 'I knew it was wrong but it wasn't all that unpleasant because he was giving me sweets. I do know I had no one to turn to. Sometimes when he came on Friday I'd lock myself in the bathroom or toilet and stay there until my mother came back. Then when I heard her close the front door I'd flush the toilet and come out. And my mother would get quite cross and tell me that old people needed company and what was I doing locking myself away? Why didn't I keep him company? But it never occurred to me to tell her. But it was the same with grandad. Once he started having intercourse I never objected, but I always felt guilty and bad. I don't know why but I always knew it was wrong. But it wasn't just that I knew it was wrong, it was also that sometimes it gave me pleasure.'

Paula told no one about her secret. One day she had caught sight of her grandfather fondling her sister. She realized then that he was doing the same things to her, and probably had been for some time. But she never mentioned it to her sister. They were both bound by their own secret and separated by a world of guilt.

When she was sixteen, Paula suddenly left home and did not contact anyone at home for over two years. She just disappeared without trace. During that period she lived in bleak rooming houses, at one time sharing rooms with local prostitutes. She became pregnant and had a horrific back-street abortion that nearly killed her. She had a series of low-paid jobs. She did not look after herself, she rarely ate, and she smoked very heavily. Finally she became critically ill and was rushed to hospital for an emergency operation. She was forced to convalesce and during that time she met her husband, whom she finally married in her late twenties after a long courtship.

There are long-term effects, although Paula feels she has overcome them. 'It took a long time for our sex life to develop,' she recalled. 'He could never understand why I was so cold. It took us even longer to have children. But we have good sex now, I've worked out my problems. But my husband has got to catch me unawares. He has learned over the years what puts me off. He never tells me to do anything or I go mad. He never caresses me or lays his fingers on me. If he were to put his fingers up my skirt or slap my bottom I would scream and throw a fit. I won't touch him and I certainly won't touch his penis at all. We just have normal sex. I did not really want to have a baby and feel I could have done something with myself if I hadn't got pregnant, but I was looking for love. But food has been my great comfort. Whenever I feel under any stress I eat. I seem to be permanently overweight.'

Paula feels she has managed her life well. But she nurses a burning resentment, not against her grandfather who assaulted her for over eight years, but against her mother for not properly looking after her or protecting her.

The long-term effects on her sister are slightly different. She began to go out with boys at thirteen and quickly became promiscuous. She has her own children but is rarely at home. She prefers to be out with one of her many men friends. Paula worries about her children, who are often abandoned in the house or left to play alone in the streets till late at night. She feels that, like their own mother, her sister is not properly protecting her children.

Paula had no one to turn to. She had a poor relationship with her mother and would not have dreamed of telling her family secret to anyone inside the family let alone outside. But it would be naive and optimistic to think that even today Paula would open up her heart to a sympathetic teacher or social worker. She might *attempt* to tell, but would anyone listen and understand?

Psychiatrists and paediatricians who are keenly aware of the terrible personal turmoil that such a child lives with have drawn up lists of warning signs in the hope that adults working with children might be more prepared to listen. When there are no bruises, burns, fractures or other unexplained injuries, abuse is difficult to imagine, let alone to talk about. If it is associated with certain behavioural disturbances, experts believe that more adults will be receptive. The lists, which are all remarkably similar, show some of the severe consequences that are currently associated with sexual abuse.

*Physical indicators*
– signs of sexually transmitted disease
– apparent pain in sitting or walking accompanied by evasive or illogical explanation
– teenage pregnancy particularly if father is unknown or secret
– somatic complaints, recurrent abdominal pain, nausea, anorexia, headache
– recurrent urinary tract infections

*Behavioural indicators*
– social withdrawal and isolation
– underachievement, distraction and day-dreaming
– fear and mistrust of those in authority, marked fear of men
– severe sleep disorders
– negative self-esteem, depression, suicidal behaviour, drug dependency
– hysterical attacks
– sexually provocative children, or those excessively preoccupied with sexual games, older girls who behave in a sexually

precocious way, sudden changes in mood
- regular avoidance and fear of medical examination
- identification with those in authority, too willing to acquiesce
  in adult demands
- model behaviour, overachievement
- regressive behaviour, like bed-wetting
- change in eating patterns, sudden faddiness, or loss of appetite

The experts insist of course that none of the signs, whether by themselves or in conjunction with others, are conclusive, and that the list is not exhaustive, but it could predispose adults working with the children to listen carefully to their stories. That in turn could be the first stage towards breaking the silence.

Once the child has been locked into the secret it is easier to accommodate it than to break away. With this in mind, Child Line was launched with great publicity towards the end of 1986 as a telephone service for children, an all-purpose help line which one of the initiators described as a Young Samaritans. The service was swamped in the first month by all different types of requests. By the second month it began to settle down to about 4,000 new referrals a month. About half of those calls came from children who claimed they were being abused or were in dangerous situations. About 1,000 said they were being sexually abused. The children wanted to talk but they did not want to be identified: they had plucked up enough courage to phone but 95 per cent of them would not give their names or addresses. So none of them could be offered any concrete support. If they were pressed to reveal their names or addresses, they immediately rang off.

Their main fear, according to Paul Griffiths, one of the directors of the project and an ex-NSPCC inspector, was that if they identified themselves they would immediately be whisked away into care or their relatives would be thrown into jail. Either way the family would be broken up and it would be seen as their fault. It would confirm their own feeling about being 'bad'.

Griffiths received one particularly dramatic call from a thirteen-year-old girl who was being raped at knifepoint regularly by her eighteen-year-old brother. She was terrified of telling her mother or father about what was happening, and yet it was clear from the enormous amount of detail she described that she was being assaulted about three times a week. She told Griffiths about one occasion when her brother had attacked her in the bathroom and she had hit her head against a towel rail and lost consciousness. When she recovered, her brother decided to take her to the doctor. At the surgery he was the model of a concerned and loving brother and did not leave her side. The doctor naturally suspected nothing, and the girl, in the menacing shadow of her brother, could tell him nothing.

This young girl insisted on remaining anonymous. Desperate though she was, she did not feel sufficiently confident to see anyone or risk standing up publicly against her brother in case he was taken away. She assumed that if that happened both her brother and her parents would turn against her and then she would have no one. According to Griffiths, the girl, and others like her, need to build up confidence before they can talk openly. The phone line might help to provide that confidence. But it might take time to reassure such children about what they are doing.

The role of the mother in cases of child sexual abuse is slightly confusing. It is claimed that most mothers are unaware of what is going on. But it also seems to be the case that some mothers refuse to know, and refuse to face up to what might be happening. Mostly they are quite aloof from the daughter concerned. But in other families the mothers clearly do know but feel that it is one way to keep the family together.

Tim Furniss, a psychiatrist working in Britain, described two types of families in a paper he wrote in 1985: 'conflict-avoiding' and 'conflict-regulating'. In the avoiding families the mother was very distant and cold in her relationship with her daughter and did not discuss any problems with her. Even if the child told the mother about a sexual approach the mother would ignore it or dismiss it. In the conflict-regulating family, the mother probably did know what was happening but was prepared to sacrifice her daughter to shore up a hopelessly antagonistic relationship. Often the mother would feel inadequate and let the child take on a mother role. In both cases the victim saw the mother as someone who did not care for her and with whom she had little or no contact.

Susie's predicament is a case in point. She was put in a foster-home at the age of twelve when the social services department discovered that her father had been sexually assaulting her. After six months she was allowed to meet her parents for a short two-hour outing one Sunday. Her parents picked her up by car and took her for a drive. That same afternoon, a policeman strolling though the car park in the local park noticed something odd going on in the back of a car. As he got nearer he saw there was a man on top of a girl having sexual intercourse. He approached to caution the couple and caught a glimpse of the girl's face. So he immediately arrested the man. The girl turned out to be Susie, the man was her father. But sitting in the front of the car all the time, staring fixedly out of the window, was Susie's mother. Could she not have known what was going on, as she claimed, or had she always colluded? Either way, she offered precious little support to her daughter.

The abusers, or the perpetrators as they are called by the professionals, evoke powerful feelings of disgust, horror and anger. Even the most sympathetic psychiatrist finds sex offenders intolerable. The group of lawyers, doctors and psychiatrists who produced *Child Sexual Abuse within the Family* argue for a more sympathetic view of incest offenders. They refer to the way Henry Giaretto, a Californian psychiatrist who has pioneered treatment for victims and their families, wrote about his first encounter with an incestuous father:

> It was a particularly raunchy case, fondling at age five, oral copulation and sodomy at eight, and full vaginal penetration at thirteen. A picture of the panic-stricken face of the girl I had just seen flashed in my brain. I was wracked by violent feelings towards the offender. I didn't want to listen to his side of the story but to kick the bastard in the crotch instead.

Since those early days, Giaretto has developed various treatment programmes and helped to set up a network of adult support groups for families.

In many states of America treatment is offered as an alternative to prison sentence. This is not considered a soft option. Offenders undergoing treatment find it extremely painful and difficult to continue. They attend because otherwise they would go to jail. It is rare for anyone actively to seek treatment.

In Britain, at Great Ormond Street Hospital, therapy was tried with families on a voluntary basis but it was found that perpetrators simply stopped attending. When they were made to attend by a court order, they submitted to regular treatment. Dr Bentovim, the head of the unit at the hospital, believes that if any treatment is to be effective the offence must stay within the criminal justice system. The difficulty for him and others working with incest offenders is to make them accept responsibility for what they have done so that the child is liberated from the guilt. But this is no easy task.

Prison alone, without treatment, has its own built-in problems. On release offenders are likely to reoffend or to commit more serious crimes. But there does seem to be a difference between those who reoffend and those who do not. Men who abuse boys are far more likely to reoffend than those who abuse girls. Those who commit incest have a low recidivism rate. But figures are difficult to compile because often incest offenders will abuse children outside the family, or alternatively have a period when they do not abuse anyone and then begin again with their grandchildren. And families are of course notorious for keeping secrets. Certainly the numbers who return home and are considered 'safe' is pathetically small. The unit at Great Ormond Street Hospital found that, due to marital break-ups, only 15 per cent of their patients lived with both parents (although 30 per cent lived with their mothers).

There are different categories of perpetrators. Some will molest children they do not know at all. Some may take weeks or months cultivating a child's friendship and building up a trusting relationship. Some will hold down extremely respectable jobs in a position of authority, like doctors or vicars or scoutmasters, and abuse the children entrusted to them. These offenders, whose victims are not members of their own families, are known as paedophiles, and tend to be more attracted to boys than girls, although they are not homosexuals in their relationship to adults.

Then there are those who abuse children within their families: fathers, stepfathers, uncles, cousins. These are known as incest offenders and tend particularly to molest girls.

The categories sometimes overlap – there are paedophiles who are also incest offenders, and there are those who begin abusing children in the family and then move to children they do not know. But most clinicians consider incest offenders different from paedophiles, although they tend to get irritated by such simplistic definitions. In Britain, those who treat one group will rarely treat the other, except in the probation service.

Ray Wyers, a consultant therapist with the probation service who has treated only sex offenders for the last ten years and has written up some of his experiences, considers that there are certain men who are quite untreatable, a view which many share. This does not mean that there should be no treatment, but that there has to be some realistic assessment to distinguish those who have a chance of being cured and those who are unlikely to be.

Wyers divides up the offenders between those who are aroused only by children and those who are aroused also by adult women or men. Paedophiles who are fixated solely on children are virtually untreatable. Some of the men he has treated claim to have had over 2,000 victims. He told us: 'You can try assertion training, victim awareness, social skills, cognitive distortions, but at the end of the day unless you can reduce their sexual arousal to children it's a waste of time. It's like alcoholism – it's addictive.' Wyers went on a tour of the USA recently looking at treatment methods but found the Americans just as pessimistic about paedophiles. One psychiatrist described the hopeless task he had of controlling men who were part of the North American Boy Love Association and who had an endless supply of contacts. He added lamely: 'Anyone who can create non-deviant arousal in paedophiles will make a fortune.'

Paedophiles do seem to get significantly more sexually aroused by children than normal men. In that meticulous way Americans have of experimenting, two different sets of researchers – K. Freund in 1976 and V. Quinsey in 1975 – tried to discover whether all men were physically excited by children. They showed three groups of men – paedophiles, heterosexuals and homosexuals – photographs of children and measured the 'penile response' to see what gave them erections. All the studies showed unequivocally that the child molesters were far more sexually excited and had greater 'penile responses' to the images of children than either heterosexual or homosexual males.

Men who commit incest are not necessarily paedophiles. They may well have normal sexual relationships with women and progress to marriage without ever being aware of any particular attraction to children. The sexual approaches are often gradual, but they become regular and are ultimately addictive. Often it involves more than one child. Once a pattern is established the father may assault all his children. He may not actively look for children outside his family network, but any child who comes under his authority could become his victim.

Wyers and other clinicians consider that incest offenders are the most promising to work with and the least likely to reoffend, providing they are identified soon enough. If they have some sexual arousal to women and are not fixated on children there is a chance that they can be cured. But this again depends on the family. If perpetrators are allowed to return home, there is always a risk of reoffending. But these risks can be assessed and monitored.

No one knows what tips the balance in a family towards incest. Marital conflicts, loss of jobs, ineffectual or inadequate sexual feelings are all cited in research and case-histories. But these are problems common to thousands of men who never sexually abuse. There does seem to be another characteristic. All the recent research has consistently found that an unusually high number of men convicted of child assault or child molesting were themselves victims. They were abused in some way when they were young and often make their victims mirror their own early experiences. Many also seem to have had some significant traumatic experience in childhood which has deeply affected them.

There is no hope of breaking the vicious cycle unless the victims tell about their experiences and receive some support and treatment early on. Punishing the offender may appear to solve the problem in the short term, but it is likely to be catastrophic for the victim, who will feel even more guilty and responsible. The appalling damage to a family cannot be eased by a prison sentence alone. There is a strong case for not prosecuting except where the public and the victims remain at risk. Certainly that is a view put forward by the Howard League for Penal Reform in a working party report, *Unlawful Sex* (1985). The number of prosecutions for neglect and cruelty is tiny. Less than fifty people each year have been tried for this offence in the last five years. Doctors, social workers and health workers have co-operated to help the families and minimize the damage. Yet sexual abuse, where the effects on the families are if anything more devastating, has not yet benefited from this approach. Treatment for the families, the offenders and the victims varies from the meagre to the non-existent.

This is not to say that sexual abuse should be decriminalized. On the contrary, all the evidence shows that only where it remains a criminal offence is there a possibility that the perpetrator will take responsibility for his actions and the victim be liberated from his or her guilt and confusion. But prosecution inevitably involves cranking up an adversarial process that in itself may distress and harm the victim further. Imprisonment alone may just harden the offender and cause terrible suffering to the child. If the child's interest is paramount, some thought has to be given to the best way of defusing the psychological time bomb.

# 8 THE SURVIVORS
## AND THE CYCLE

One of the myths about the suffering of children, which has comforted the adult world, is that young bodies and young minds heal quickly, that most abused children recover from their experiences and go on to be happy men and women, able to function normally in the community.

But as our society has come to admit more about family violence it has become clear that a badly damaged child often grows into a badly damaged adult. Our easy assumption that terrible trauma may be erased just by the passage of time is destroyed by the evidence of victims, now grown up, who are prepared to look back and face the impact which their childhood experiences have had on the rest of their lives.

But perhaps what is most depressing for those who study patterns of child abuse and, more especially, for those who have the task of managing practical cases, is the realization that, in families where any form of abuse has begun and apparently come to be accepted, there seems to be an almost inevitable repetition of this type of behaviour from one generation to the next. A child who is neglected, or more positively abused, whether emotionally, sexually or physically, seems to carry that abuse, like a curse, into adult life, and to be almost driven to inflicting some kind of abuse on his or her own children. An adult who appears to survive early personal abuse almost always has a burden of anger and guilt which is most visibly expressed in recurring violence and, invisibly, in internal psychological struggles with his or her own emotions. The common-sense view that a parent who has been battered as a child might consciously and conscientiously strive not to reproduce that suffering in his or her own family is denied by nearly every case-book, where the abusing mother or father is almost always discovered to have been an abused child. It is tempting to conclude that this cycle suggests the inevitability of malevolent fate, and it is not surprising that professional workers in this field sometimes despair of breaking into an apparently remorseless sequence of abuse creating abuse from one generation to the next.

The dismal history of the Broadbent family could be told from the viewpoint of any one of the four generations who live today in the Nottingham area, all of whose lives have been in some way blighted by a chain of abuse. We have learned most about twenty-three-year-old Carol Broadbent who, very recently, has seemed willing to acknowledge and to try and resolve some of the 'fateful' patterns of her own inheritance. She has had some expert help in attempting to free herself from that inheritance, but it may already be too late for her own son Nicky, who seems, at seven years old, destined to grow up as yet another abused abuser.

Carol was born in 1963, when her father Ian was eighteen years old and her mother Edna sixteen. They had married when Edna was five months pregnant. Both she and Ian came from large, disorganized families where violence had been sufficiently bad for the local social services to be aware of domestic difficulties and crises in both households long before the two teenagers became parents. Carol's own earliest memories are of violence: 'My father was very violent with my mother, and he was always getting into fights. He used to get ever so drunk. He's been to prison quite a few times for grievous bodily harm, and just general fighting and violence. A very violent man. I've always been surrounded by violence.'

Edna Broadbent had two more babies, and then in the summer of 1969, when Carol was six, she escaped from her battering husband and went off to London, leaving the three young children behind. All of them went into foster care, but Carol's paternal grandmother took her in. A few months later, Edna, having established a new relationship with a man in London, took the younger two south to live with her. Edna's new partnership has endured over the years; she has had another child and provided a stable home for the children. But, although Carol's brother and sisters have been happy with their mother, she still feels deeply betrayed by Edna, both for her initial disappearance and because she was left with her grandmother when the others went to join their mother. Carol and her mother have never formed a satisfactory connection, and now that Carol is able to look more objectively at her feelings and emotions, she thinks that many of her own problems over the years have stemmed from this unsatisfactory relationship, which was itself directly caused by her father's violence.

'I can't look on her as a mother as such because she wasn't there when I needed her. We see each other once or twice a year but we don't really have much contact. I can't ever forgive her for taking my brother and sister to London and leaving me. She had the chance to take me as well and she didn't and that's the most upsetting part of it. I've had countless arguments with my mother over the years, saying, "Why didn't you take me as well as them?" But she always said that my dad wanted me and so she let him have me.'

Edna Broadbent saw her decision to leave Carol in Nottingham as a simple practical solution for her divided family, particularly as her elder daughter had already been absorbed into her in-laws' home before she was ready to take her other children out of care. To Carol the pain of apparently being rejected by her mother has been immeasurably compounded by the traumatic experiences of life with her grandparents – their home was not the sanctuary that both the child and her mother had believed.

'My dad's father, my grandfather, was having incest with one of his daughters, my Auntie Eileen, and I had a lot of trouble because he tried to do the same with me while I was living under the same roof as the rest of them. But he never actually made love to me because I wouldn't let him but he did try quite a lot of times. I didn't really know what to do. I just knew myself that it was wrong what he was trying to do. My grandfather worked down the pit and my grandmother used to work at a public house, working in the afternoons and at nights. But while she was working my grandfather used to get drunk – it only happened when he was drunk. So, when he came back from the pub before my grandma did, I used to sit on the wall outside and wait for her. They had a little wall surrounding the house, you see, because it was an end house, but it had a massive garden and I used to sit on the fence waiting for my grandma to come in, to keep away from him as much as I could. And sometimes I'd sit on the wall till about one o'clock in the morning till she came in, but I wouldn't go into the house because I was just too afraid of him. I once told my grandma about it and she went down to my grandad's allotment to see him and he said he hadn't touched me and my grandma just came back and said that my grandad hadn't touched me and that was it. Nothing more was said about it.'

Eventually the police intervened, turning a less blind eye to Mr Broadbent senior's activities than his wife had done. Carol's grandfather was charged with, and later jailed for, incest with his own adolescent daughter Eileen. It never emerged that he had persistently molested the much younger granddaughter, but at this point Edna, hearing the story from afar, decided that it was unsuitable for Carol to remain in the household and successfully applied for her daughter to come and live with her. But now that her grandfather had been removed from the scene, nine-year-old Carol had no wish to leave the cosy familiarity of the pit village to be with her estranged mother, her brother and sister, and a new stepfather and stepsister who, by this time, were all living in Dagenham, Essex. So she went very reluctantly, in spite of her initial anger at being left behind.

Carol seems to have disrupted the entire Dagenham household, refusing to accept any discipline from her stepfather, quarrelling with her mother and siblings, and constantly demanding that she be allowed to go back to Nottingham. After three years Edna gave in and Carol returned to her grandparents' house under a supervision order held by the local county council. It was a strange family setting for the child: Ian, her father, had just been released from a prison sentence for grievous bodily harm, and grandad had come home after serving his two-year sentence for incest. However, Carol insists that there were no further attempts to assault her sexually after the reunion and, apart from the usual drunken brawls and various incidents when Ian hit Carol for truancy, life seems to have settled into a relatively stable pattern.

Two years later there was another major disruption when

Ian Broadbent suddenly remarried and Carol was once more uprooted into another household, this time with her father, a stepmother and the stepmother's children. Carol had to join a new secondary school in the third year and found it very difficult to fit in. Her truancy got worse and there were reports that she was stealing both at school and from local shops. She did not settle happily with her stepmother, and neither did her father. After a few months he began to beat his new wife, Linda, just as he had beaten Edna years before. Soon the repetition of the pattern was carried to its conclusion and, after only fifteen months of marriage, Linda left. Carol was, once again, alone with her father who, once again, said he could not cope with her and turned to his parents for help. But this time the local social services authorities, aware of Mr Broadbent senior's record of incest, decided that the fourteen-year-old Carol would be morally unsafe in her grandfather's house, and she was taken into care. No one knew about the earlier abuse and so it was only Carol who saw the irony of being removed at this point from a danger that she had already confronted at a much more tender age. Her resentment and frustration were intense.

Carol was sent first to one and then to another temporary foster-home and it was at this stage that the cumulative uncertainty and trauma of her childhood seemed to erupt in her adolescent life. The festering, confused emotions exploded in reckless shoplifting, promiscuity and then repeated overdosing on paracetamol and aspirin, any drug which she could easily buy. Asked to leave various foster-homes, she was sent to an adolescent assessment centre and then to a community home in Mansfield. The reports of her time there make alarming reading:

Carol causes the staff considerable concern; she has shown herself a compulsive liar, she becomes hysterical at any reprimand, and has staged pathetic suicide attempts and displayed superb dramatic scenes for the benefit of anyone handy. We have tried to help Carol in every way, but she seems not to respond to warmth and affection, the things she said she needed. She did begin to go out with a boy from school, Paul Monger. She caused him much distress and unhappiness over her possessiveness. When his affections cooled she displayed further attempts at mock suicide.

Eventually she realized that she had no chance of regaining his friendship and, within days, she was continuing a previous courtship with another boy. Floods of emotional letters have supported her feelings and her purpose at the moment is to 'care and love Dale', the boy. Carol was released from school to do one week's work programme at a department store in Mansfield. Whilst there she stole twelve pounds from her training staff member and various articles from the department she worked in. She was found out but the police have not prosecuted.

Three months later the community home despaired:

Over a short period of time Carol's behaviour has deteriorated to such an extent that we feel we can't contain her and give her the structured firm environment she needs to overcome her lack of self-control and help her mature without the repercussions of many problems she now faces. A recent incident supports our decision. Carol absconded on January 19th and was missing for six days. Her first night was spent in the basement of a carpark with two young men. She knew the boys only that evening, both had sexual intercourse with her. They parted company in the morning and Carol went to visit one of her aunties. During the afternoon Carol was picked up by David Cartwright, an eighteen-year-old boy on probation. Carol then went straight with David to stay with his married sister. She remained there until the following Thursday, and during this time had sexual intercourse with the intention of getting pregnant as David had said he would marry her.

At this time Carol was fifteen and a half years old. All the evidence suggests that the adults who came into contact with her, and who were professionally responsible for her welfare, tried very hard to find ways of helping her. There were numerous case conferences which included her schoolteachers as well as the residential staff of the community home and social workers. Emissaries were sent to Edna in Essex to see if there was any way in which she could now provide a stable home for her eldest child, but Edna pleaded ill-health and recalled the disruption Carol had caused four years before. Ian Broadbent was still living a single, drunken, violent existence and it had already been decided that his family were unsuitable guardians. The tone of many of the reports and assessments on Carol at this time suggests precisely the sense of official frustration in the face of 'inexorable tragedy' that we have already described as common in dealing with similar families.

At one stage, after three episodes of overdosing in as many weeks, Carol was sent to a clinical psychiatrist for consultation and possible treatment. His report reflects the typical attitudes of those who came into contact with Carol; the solution to some of her problems seemed obvious but unattainable and her emotional state had reached an intractable point. 'My clinical impression', wrote the doctor,

> is that Carol is a physically mature girl who has had prolonged emotional deprivation, and virtually no consistent emotional relationship since the age of six. I do not feel that there is any definite psychiatric treatment that can help Carol; her present needs are a secure home environment where she can build up trusting relationships. Carol has had such disruptive and damaging experiences in the past, with little on the positive side, that I think she is quite badly damaged. I did discuss with the social worker the possibility of her admission to the Regression Unit that the Social Services run, but I was doubtful about this as Carol is a bit old to start on such a course. I have not made any arrangements to follow up Carol as an outpatient.

After much deliberation the social services decided to try and settle Carol in a special halfway house for disturbed adolescents in Coventry. Here it was felt she would be far away from all the conflicting and generally negative influences of her family and old friends, would be able to train for a job, and would also be given the individual attention and therapy which had been impossible in an ordinary community home. At first it all seemed to go surprisingly well. Carol began to help in a children's nursery and relished the experience. She accepted domestic responsibilities in the home and seemed to calm down emotionally – there were no more suicide attempts.

Carol herself remembers her time in Coventry enthusiastically: 'I enjoyed it there. You had to share cleaning up in the morning, and you had to take turns cooking the dinner and shopping. There were all kinds of plans and things like that. I enjoyed it quite a lot. I had lots of friends there who were willing to help me and the social services were willing to help. But then during that period of time I caught my son Nicky.'

Carol only discovered she was pregnant after three and a half months and her account of being told vividly reveals the pathos of this apparently sophisticated yet vulnerable sixteen-year-old. 'I'd been to the doctor's with stomach pains. You see, I was actually on the pill but the doctors just gave them to me without explaining to me what you do with them. So really I was only taking them when I was actually making love. I left a specimen of water with the doctor who said I'd probably got a bug or something. Then I got a phone call asking me to go down to the office. It was about quarter to eight in the morning and I was getting ready to go to my nursery teaching class. The doctor told me to sit down and he said that, you know, I was pregnant. It was a very, very big shock. I was just off in a daze, all that day. And then I got back to the house at night, and by then the doctor had told them, and there was a big meeting about it, including my boyfriend Mark, who was my son's dad, but we'd really finished by then. It was said that I couldn't remain in Coventry, not being pregnant – they just wasn't able to cope with pregnant ladies, you see. It was just a hostel for adolescent people, not for pregnant women or anything like that.'

The possibility of abortion was raised but Carol dismissed it. There was no hope of creating a permanent relationship with the discarded Mark and so the only alternative was for her to return to yet another foster-home in her home area to await the birth of the baby. Carol's farewell reports from Coventry were pessimistic:

Our major concern is that this pregnancy will wipe out all the progress she has made here. It is extremely unlikely that she will be able to cope with a child. She herself has recognized that she lacks patience and wonders if the baby upsets her if she'll be able to control her feelings. On one occasion she said she could see herself as a battering mother. She has a great deal of growing up to do and we do not see how this process can be completed in view of the present situation.

Carol's own solution to her immediate problems was in line with her past behaviour. In a few months she had started a relationship with her foster-parents' son and in June 1981 she celebrated her wedding to Peter Maybury in the same month as her son Nicky's first birthday. Carol was released from care when she married, although she was not yet eighteen, and like her mother began life as a teenage wife with the additional responsibility of a child to look after. The parallels with the previous generation bleakly continued when soon after the marriage Peter began to hit his bride, to come home drunk, and to create domestic havoc for Carol and Nicky. After just over a year of sickeningly familiar violence Carol left her husband.

Today, six years later, Carol, at twenty-four, is, perhaps surprisingly, still a resilient girlish woman with long, dark, wavy hair and an easy, friendly smile. She now has four children and lives in her own council flat on a bleak housing estate on the outskirts of Nottingham. Two more men called Peter have come into her life since she left her husband. The first post-marital Peter fathered her daughter Sandra, who is now three and a half years old, and then she took up with the father of the younger children – Suzanne, who is eighteen months, and baby Joanna.

Carol and 'third Peter' have now been living together for over four years and Carol hopes it will go on, although there have been major rifts between them: 'We've been going through some difficult phases. I've had to put my son Nicky into care now and Peter says that if Nicky comes back he'll leave permanently. I had to put Nicky into care because we've had lots of bad times with Nicky. He was setting fires, stealing from shops, excreting all over his bedroom. Totally destructive in every possible way. Anything that Peter had he would wreck, his calculator he ripped to pieces. He burned the video unit because he couldn't have a film on that he wanted. So after I went in to have Joanna in hospital he went into foster care and he hasn't come back. So now I'm in a difficult position because I'm torn between the two, the love of my son and the love of my two children's father. I explained to the social worker that it's probably better to put Nicky in long-term care for the simple reason that I'm going through a very bad stage myself. I'm just able to cope with the children I've got at the moment. So having Nicky back is quite low on the list.'

Nicky was already on the at-risk register before he went into care. His schoolteacher had noticed violent red bruise marks on his neck, and Carol admitted that she had grabbed him and shaken him because he was so difficult to handle. She has now told the social workers that one of the reasons she wants Nicky to stay away is that she cannot trust herself not to be more violent with him if he is with her all the time. Perhaps in one way Carol is lucky, because her problems have been so acute that she has stayed closely in touch with the local social services, and seems uninhibited about turning to them for advice and practical help. Unlike many young parents whose own experiences lead them to abuse their own children, Carol does not feel isolated from any kind of support. One social worker is now giving Carol regular counselling and through this she has been able recently to express and partially come to terms with some of the events and emotions of her childhood, and to see the repercussions on her present life. The professionals hope that this may make it possible for her somehow to break out of the abusing patterns she inherited.

'I've just been able to think about what happened,' Carol explains, 'because I've had a social worker come every week on a Tuesday and I've started talking it through with her, because I've had so many feelings about it all for so long and I just kept them all to myself. No one's ever known about my grandad trying to make love to me because I never said anything. But I had so much anger and frustration all pent up for so many years that I had to talk to someone even though it was so long ago. All that with my grandad has affected my relationships with any man I've been with – the physical side of it has always been very strained. It's just the way I react to people, especially men. I've always been a bit afraid of them. Even now I still find a lot of difficulty relating to the children's father physical-wise. It would help a lot if I could actually speak to my grandma about my grandad. I'd like to ask her why she let it happen and why she couldn't have done something for me. But it's so hard because my grandad's died of cancer now and I think it would hurt her too much.

'I never think of my father fondly. If you'd have asked me quite a few years ago I would have said yes, but I look at it as that he's the person what made me as I was, what put me in my

position in the first place, because if he'd have kept going to
work and he hadn't been violent towards my mum, perhaps
they would have still been together. I mean, perhaps they
wouldn't have been, but at least my mother wouldn't have had
to have left him. I did blame my mother for a long, long time,
but as I've grown older I've realized that no woman should be
left in a house where she'll stay in a position where she's being
beaten all the time. So I don't blame my mother for leaving. But
I have started to think a lot about my father. I blame him for a
lot of things. I mean, I could have stayed with him and my
stepmother. I didn't really like my stepmother very much, his
second wife, but I think I would have stuck it out if he hadn't
have started hitting her as well. See, wherever I've gone or
whatever home I've made he's destroyed it in so many different
ways. Like he made a new life for himself, he made a new
family for himself and then totally destroyed it.'

Carol's social-work counsellor is now trying gently to point
out to her that she, in her turn, may be destroying her son
Nicky's security by her own violence and by her decision to send
him away to foster care. Nicky is almost exactly the same age
as Carol was when her mother Edna abandoned her, and the
signs that he is already disturbed are painfully obvious in his
behaviour. But Carol may also, consciously or unconsciously,
be looking at the other lessons of her mother's life which have
produced for Edna a much happier middle age than might
have seemed possible from her early, violent marriage. Edna
deliberately chose to give higher priority to her relationship
with a new partner than to the needs of her eldest child, and by
doing so she succeeded in providing a settled home for herself
and her other children. Carol herself has now been sterilized
and feels that without the disruptive presence of Nicky she can
care adequately for her little girls, and she wants their father to
stay with her.

Everyone who has talked to Carol now recognizes that,
although she suffered badly from the initial trauma of separation
from her mother, it was her subsequent experiences which
prevented any chance she might have had of maturing in a stable
environment as an unscarred adult. Now it is being suggested
that Nicky may indeed be better off away from his natural
mother, and that, if a long-term foster or adopting home can be

found, it may still be possible to break him out of the generational pattern of abuse by helping him develop emotional ties with other, non-related adults. It may be too late, but if the 'bonds of barbed wire' between Carol and Nicky can be broken then both may eventually not only survive their own experiences of abuse but shatter the previously apparently inevitable cycle which has haunted the Broadbent family.

The key to any possible optimism about Carol and Nicky is that their problems have been so acute that, even at what may be a very late stage, they are getting active help in trying to deal with them. There are many other survivors of child abuse who have had to struggle on alone, battling with the unresolved angers that their earlier miseries produce.

Pamela Morgan, who is fifteen years older than Carol, grew up in a generation where professional awareness and understanding of the battered child was limited and primitive. Pamela's parents held their fragile household together. The child was never taken into care, her condition was never recognized, and, as she grew up, she repressed her memories and has been unable to understand or cope with the many troubles of her adult life.

Today, on the telephone at a distance, Pamela sounds exactly the sort of person she has fought so hard to become: a mature, secure woman with a well-established home and family. She talks confidently of her teenage son and daughter, of her community work with battered wives, of her successful relationship with a partner whose childhood polio has left him disabled. There was nothing in the way she speaks of her present, comfortable, if challenging, life to suggest that Pamela spent her childhood in almost total degradation, forced by a brutal father into a squalid, animal-like existence. She eventually escaped from her father by being clever, by going to college, but the more you know Pamela the more you understand how close she really still is to her horrific childhood; her scars are deep and permanent. Physically, the first thing you notice when you meet her in person is that she has only one eye, the other having been lost in a family fight when she was sixteen. The psychological scars are superficially hidden, but, when revealed, are just as disfiguring. Pamela has never truly escaped her battered childhood. She has only survived.

Our first contact with Pamela came through a long and frighteningly vivid letter she wrote to us about her early memories. It was an extraordinary letter obviously written by an educated person, describing life in London in the late 1950s and 1960s, and yet painting a picture of Dickensian misery, drunkenness and abuse. Pamela was born in 1948, the same year as the National Health Service. By the time she went to primary school the welfare state with all its armoury of social security and protective agencies was in full swing. None of it seemed to touch this family. Pamela was the eldest of five children – three boys and two girls – who existed in three damp and cold rooms in Paddington, where enormous mushroom fungi grew on the walls and drains overflowed into the house. Both Pamela's parents had jobs: her father worked as a tailor's cutter; her mother was a very efficient shorthand typist. From the outside they may have appeared a hard-working, competent family with no need of social support, but inside their basement flat they lived in a way which would have been familiar to deprived children a century before.

My father drank. I don't know if he was an alcoholic – I suspect he was, but I was too young to know. He drank nearly all his wages away. To say that we were underfed and poorly clothed is an understatement. We were practically starving. I realize as I write that we never had curtains. We had no hot water, and only a broken toilet that had to be flushed by bucket. I said my father drank – this was his only real occupation in life. He was hardly ever at home but when he was he made us suffer. There was a nightly scramble to be in bed before he came home from the pub. When he came home he would bolt and bar the door trapping us inside, then come round each bed and shine a torch in each sleeping person's face. We all pretended to be asleep; it was the safest tactic. He would also feel all the light bulbs to see if we were truly asleep.

Quite often, especially at weekends, we children would be got out of bed to hear our sins. He would start on my mother, hitting her where she lay, in order to get her up. He would then make her get the rest of us up. We would then be lined up in the kitchen in order of age, while we were cross-questioned. He would stride up and down the line ranting and raving, often hitting us for not standing straight or rubbing a nose or whatever. Anyone who showed any signs of fear was automatically guilty and beaten right away. Usually he wanted one of us to 'own up' before punishing us and just gave us a few preliminary whacks to 'get the truth out'. By picking on one of us he could get that child to incriminate the others. My father cursed us so much and heaped so much verbal abuse on us that I learned only one new swear-word after the age of eleven. My father always swore that he was 'fair in his chastisement', that he always hit us with his open hand and not his fist, but we were sometimes punched, knocked to the floor and kicked and spat on. I remember one of the teachers at school commenting on my brother's black eye when he was seven.

The alert teacher may have reported this incident because Pamela remembers that about this time an NSPCC inspector came to the flat. The children hoped that this would bring some relief but their father was too cunning to allow the authorities to get anywhere near the truth. He showed the children's excellent school reports and spoke of their high intelligence and wonderful behaviour. The children themselves were hidden away, listening behind a door to the conversation about the reports (ruefully reflecting that these were the same reports which had earlier brought about severe beatings because they were judged unsatisfactory), but not daring to speak to the inspector themselves. The NSPCC officer went away, and although he called again, he never insisted on meeting the children and hearing their side of the story – a mistake which has been made over and over again by generations of well-meaning people trying to investigate complicated cases of child abuse.

It is hard for Pamela, and for anyone hearing her story, to know what might have been best for her, and her brothers and sisters, if any outside authority had known how they were treated and been able to intervene. At that time the most usual decision would have been to place all the children in residential care. The family would probably have been broken up between different institutions. Today most experts would deplore the loss of family connections but Pamela is realistic about the relationships with her own siblings and feels there was little to value in having brothers and a sister.

> You must understand that living in the atmosphere we did, we were infected by it almost as if it were a disease. There was no solidarity between us children, no love between us. We treated each other in the same way that he treated us. We beat each other over trivial slights, asserted claims over certain toys, broke others to get even, blackmailed each other by threatening to tell my father of imaginary misdeeds. We were constantly in conflict and fought at the slightest provocation. The only response we knew was violence. We would often accuse one another at my father's behest to divert a beating from ourselves. Whether we did wrong, or whether we did right, the result was always the same – a beating. We lived in constant fear when my father was around and went wild when he wasn't.

Common sense suggests that even the most sanguine modern supporter of family preservation would find it difficult to identify many virtues in this particular nuclear unit; united only by biology, they were viciously at war in every part of everyday life. And yet there were elements in the relationship between Pamela and her father which were in a strange way constructive, and which allowed her to develop the strength to oppose him, and, eventually, to leave.

As she got older, Pamela's intelligence lifted her out of her miserable background. She passed the eleven-plus and went to Maida Vale Grammar School; she won school prizes and played in the orchestra. Some of these distinctions seemed to focus her father's attention and fury more especially on her and she remembers incidents which appeared to be stimulated by his irritation at her success.

> One Saturday afternoon I was alone with my father and he started on about something, I forget what, and when I denied it I was called a liar, the usual routine. This time it went further and he demanded that I swear on the Bible that I was telling the truth. So I got my Bible, a cherished school prize, and swore on it that I was telling the truth. Far from ending my troubles, the appearance of the Bible seemed to

provoke my father to a frenzy of rage and he beat me round the face with an old bone shoe horn for being such a terrible hypocritical liar. I had already been beaten before producing my Bible, and I remember swearing with tears streaming down my cheeks and such a lump in my throat that I could hardly speak. I don't remember how it ended but when my mother came in I was in bed exhausted. My mother asked my father what he had been doing and for once he was rather shamefaced and quiet. My mother took me round to the doctor and showed him my bruises. When we got home again my father had gone out. I was rather dazed and couldn't believe what had happened to me.

Once she had recovered her equanimity, the growing girl was fired by these terrible incidents, not cast down into defeated, depressed acceptance of her lot as her mother had been. She hated her father with an energetic anger which gave her the ambition not only to defeat him but to protect the other members of the family. Pamela still breaks down in tears, twenty-five years later, when she talks about her recognition, early in her teens, that her fear had been transformed into anger, and that her frustration at being physically overwhelmed could be soothed by besting her father in arguments.

I would stand up to my father and argue with him, and he would rage for ages, often into the small hours of the morning. I could see right through his feeble logic and enjoyed taking him on in these ridiculous sessions. I did have a point though to my almost suicidal tactics. If my father was trying to prove me wrong, he was not beating my mother or brothers. At first my mother would hover around uncertainly but eventually she used to leave us to it. Usually if I was hit during these sessions it was only once or twice and I didn't run away but stood my ground. Occasionally I misjudged the tempo and my father would beat me with fury, knocking me down with a rain of blows. Then I would crawl to bed in the dark, sobbing my heart out, and my mother, who would already be hiding in her bed, would say, 'I don't know why you do it, I really don't.' I did it because someone had to stand up to him. It's like the concentration camps: it's somebody to hate that keeps you going because that's your whole driving force.

Pamela does not know how she would have handled this adolescent rage and hatred if she had been removed from her father,
placed with foster-parents or in a children's home. Some experts
argue that if she had been less angry, perhaps lulled into
indifference in more tranquil surroundings, she might have
achieved less. The difficult question is to assess how much she
really did achieve by aggressively taking on the challenge of
defending herself in the best way she could. No one offered her
any professional advice or guidance and she simply allowed her
overwhelming anger to direct her teenage years.

The determination to regard her home as a concentration
camp, to be triumphed over and escaped from, carried Pamela
through successful o-levels and into the grammar school sixth
form. It sustained her during the long, traumatic hospital treatment when her left eye had to be removed after a violent struggle
with her young brother. Eventually she was accepted at a teacher
training college in Lancashire, chosen she says because it was as
far away as possible from Paddington. Predictably, her father
opposed her going to college, told her she should get a proper
job and for a while managed to obstruct her grant applications.
But, by now, Pamela's mother, perhaps affected by her daughter's example, was helping her attempts to break away and
supported her both practically and emotionally. So, in 1966,
Pamela went off optimistically to the northern college, thinking
that the black terrible childhood could be permanently buried
and that adult life would begin with a completely new start.
Nothing would be carried with her from the brutality of the
basement flat.

Now, aged thirty-nine, Pamela is just beginning to acknowledge that it has not been like that. She is beginning to accept
that the burden of being an abused child has weighed heavily
on her for all of the last twenty years. Her family have created
a conspiracy of silence about 'the bad times'. Pamela is on quite
good terms with her mother, who was widowed several years
ago and now lives a vigorous life involved in community politics
only two miles from her old home. But mother and daughter
never speak of the past or discuss the man who tried to destroy
both their lives. Pamela's brothers have been in trouble with the

law and the bottle but they too never look back at the roots of their problems and have not talked to their sister about their mutual suffering and mutual hostility. They bully the women in their lives and have done little except drift on the fringes of society. No one except for an occasional probation officer or policeman has ever begun to look at the background of their family life or been able to explain what a legacy is usually left by a brutal childhood.

During our conversations with Pamela, she felt able for the first time to face the whole story of her childhood, and she finds it extremely painful to relate any of those early experiences to her present life. We are obviously not professional counsellors or therapists, but it was clear that even informal, open discussions with two journalists released tensions and pent-up anxieties that Pamela has been struggling with alone. Her determination to hide and conceal the past, which she feels deeply ashamed of, has been as fierce and self-protective as her previous anger against her father. Since she was a young girl, Pamela's apparent strength has made her difficult to help, resistant to approaches that could reveal her underlying vulnerability. Now that she is older and has fought a lone battle with many of the external and internal crises that have beset her, she is coming to terms with the scars of her childhood and is more receptive to an analysis of the past which means aggravating those scars again. The tragedy is that long ago there was no one in the welfare or education system who was able to reach out to the suffering damaged child who has now become a damaged woman.

The first year that Pamela spent away from her family was, in a different way, as much a nightmare as life at home had been. She arrived at the teacher training college overjoyed at the thought of student life, but she was totally unprepared to cope with bedsitter freedom and, as she says, 'fell immediately and completely off the rails'. Within three months she had spent her grant in the local pubs and was pregnant by a casual boyfriend who certainly had no interest in a baby. Pamela returned to London in a distraught state and tried to get an abortion but, like so many unsophisticated girls of that era, she was defeated by the legal requirement that two psychiatrists should certify that the pregnancy was a threat to her mental health. Ironically her consultations brought her close to psychiatric treatment when one doctor she saw considered her mentally disturbed and admitted her to hospital. But as soon as she discovered that this hospital was not going to perform an abortion, Pamela discharged herself. She ended up having neither the abortion nor the mental therapy that might have eased the complications of her life.

Pamela had the baby, her son James now aged twenty, arranged to take a year off from college and became a hippie.

> I took vast quantities of drugs and made money by street
> trading – beads, bells, furry animals; it was 1967 and
> everything exploded in London. I'd go up to Soho in the
> evening, mini-skirt up to my knickers, but I was never
> molested because I was basically part of the scene. I wasn't
> frightened because I thought I could defend myself and
> anyway I was really too stoned to know what was going on.

Pamela visited her mother and took care to avoid seeing her father, but she replaced him with a boyfriend whom she married, and who seemed to have some familiar characteristics. Phil was fifteen years older than Pamela, he was a very heavy drinker and tried to dominate her with violence. Phil, Pamela and the baby went back to Lancashire, where Pamela decided, despite the haze of marijuana, that she must resume her training. The marriage lasted only a few months; Pamela saw through Phil in the same way that she had seen through her father. He was less clever than her and she despised his stupidity. She was now twenty, with a broken marriage, an illegitimate baby and a potentially serious addiction to drugs and to alcohol. It looked as though, in spite of her ambition, Pamela was unable to escape the imprint of instability and violence. But again she decided to suppress her problems, and, leaving James with a babysitter, finished her course.

The next big hurdle for Pamela was to try work as a teacher. Once again she found she could not cope.

> I couldn't take the atmosphere of the staffroom, I just didn't
> know how to behave. I'd never learned how to have a
> conversation, how to get on with anybody in an ordinary
> way. I'd certainly never learned it at home, never learned it

as a hippie, and after that I isolated myself with the baby. So
I didn't know what to do and yet I couldn't take being
invisible in the staffroom, I couldn't take not being
acknowledged by the headmaster. I just couldn't take their
bloody system. The kids were alright but I wasn't able to
cope with all the other teachers.

Pamela gave up the post and has never worked as a teacher
again. The professional training she had fought for at school
and then doggedly returned to after her first disastrous student
year has not been enough to overcome the personal and social
handicaps inflicted on her as a child.

But while her professional life came to a halt, Pamela seemed
to have better luck in her relations with a man. She met Christopher, the husband of one of her girlfriends, and started
what she now discreetly describes as a 'liaison'. She admired
Christopher, a graduate who could match her in brain-power.
Again he was older than her but he did not seem to seek
automatic domination. Christopher's most obvious physical
characteristic is a calipered leg, the result of crippling infantile
paralysis. Pamela now thinks there was some instinctive sympathy and attraction between herself and another young person
with a startling disability. After a time, there were some fairly
civilized marital rearrangements and Christopher and Pamela
set up home. Sixteen years later, they are still together. Although
they have never married, they have a daughter, fifteen-year-old
Sophie, and it is this partnership which now dominates Pamela's
life.

Superficially there seems little to link Christopher and Pamela's household with her childhood home. They live in a comfortable house looking out on to the moors on the outskirts of
Chorley in Lancashire, by chance close to the college that Pamela
attended. Christopher works in computer software, James has
just left home to train as a nurse and Sophie does well at her
secondary school, but all their lives are still affected by Pamela's
old unresolved anger and by her instinct to handle problems
with violence. Perhaps it is psychologically inevitable that Christopher should turn out to be another damaged person with
deep-seated difficulties that he never has been helped to deal with.

Soon after Pamela began to live with Christopher she found

that he had a violent temper:

> He's got absolutely no control of his temper. He created this
> whole aura of violence, because he would go wild and start
> throwing things around. I would shout at him and argue just
> like I did with my father and everyone would be crying and
> bellowing; the kids would be crying and everyone would be
> running and hiding, and Chris not exactly breaking things
> up but we got through an awful lot of china. The pair of us
> were just bound to do it the wrong way. If I didn't shout
> back when he lost his temper I took the part of being the
> snivelling wretch, crying just like my mother. It was just like
> all the echoes of my past, loud voices, loud bangs, shouting,
> slam the doors. I began to have terrible nightmares, and
> Chris and I both started to hit James. When things went
> wrong with us, James tended to get blamed for everything
> and we would both take it out on him. I think it it went on
> for about five years and, by then, we were beating Sophie
> as well.

As we have shown, the pattern of abused children becoming
abusing parents is so common that many experts now consider
it a high-risk factor in assessing families. One of the problems
for social services agencies handling child-abuse cases is that the
family history is often not available and that investigation in
this sensitive area may totally destroy trust. The academic and
anecdotal evidence is clear: whether the parents have experienced abuse must be established, and if they have it must be
recognized as an important danger signal which can help in
avoiding threats to the next generation of children. Pamela,
Chris and their children were never under any social-work care
and had to struggle on, dealing with their violence entirely on
their own.

The whole family might have spiralled downwards in a
ghastly replay of the previous generation but once again Pamela's peculiar capacity for self-protection emerged and she used
her old weapons of intelligence and energy to try and improve
her life. Through a series of accidental connections, she got
involved in local community work and was then offered a job
in a refuge for battered wives. It was run by a group of women
with a strong feeling of sisterhood and they offered insights and

support that Pamela had never had, as well as the professional status she craved and felt was her due. Sadly the job did not last long, because Pamela, afflicted by her recurring self-doubt, became so stressed that she found it impossible to carry on. But the lessons of dealing with other people's domestic violence caused her to take an analytic look at her own home life. She appealed to Chris to discuss it with her and seems by her own account to have succeeded in dealing with some of the problems in a rational, intellectual way. They took a joint decision to stop hitting the children, and stuck to it; and they resolved to look for friends and companions outside the family, to try and break their lonely claustrophobic pattern of life. But Pamela has found it very difficult to expand her horizons. In the same way that she longs to be able to hold down a responsible, fulfilling job, she wants to be able to associate easily with people, to be an accepted player in middle-class life, but at every turn she is consciously and unconsciously held back. Today she feels that the very worst thing her father did to her was to isolate her socially:

> I had no uncles or aunts or cousins or anything; we had no friends and it was really bad. I didn't realize at the time how bad it was to cut us off so completely even from our grandfather. It did more damage than anything else, because the only thing we learned was to shout, to rave, to hit people, you solve all problems by coercion and by threats, and all we knew was this terrible way of behaviour.

Pamela doesn't shout or rave at her Chorley neighbours and on the whole her family is calm. But she still has not been able to find and hold on to a satisfactory job, is on uncertain terms with the outside world and is constantly apprehensive about destructive anger sparked either by Chris or by herself. The veneer of stable maturity is alarmingly fragile.

Pamela's first letter to us ended suddenly with an abrupt note: 'I apologize for the amount of material,' she wrote, 'but once I started writing, I couldn't stop. Then I was so affected by what I had written that I did have to stop writing, because I couldn't sleep at night. I was getting up at two or three in the morning because I could not rest or find any comfort in my bed.' The narrative of her childhood had stopped at no obvious point, but much later, when we talked, Pamela explained why she had gone no further.

> I was at the point where even though I wanted to say this I couldn't actually put it down. Where we lived in the basement, there was a point in the passage where I used to stand and look through a skylight above the front door which was always bolted and barred so that we were actually locked in. Through the skylight I could see across the road to houses on the other side, and there was one that never drew its curtains, and there was always a light on, and I could stand there in the dark and look at this lighted window and that used to keep me feeling safe. That was my security for a long time. I was going to put that down in the letter but it really affects me because it's been suppressed for years. I thought I could handle it but when I started to write it I was dreadful. I was simply dreadful, I sat down and just sort of got the shakes. I was terrible for days and days afterwards because it all came back and I was suffering just the same.

Pamela is an abused child who has survived. To the outside world she is a remarkable woman who has struggled to create a successful, normal life, but to herself she is still the frightened angry little girl who desperately hypnotized herself with a comforting light in the street.

# 9  THE DUTCH SOLUTION

The Dutch have their own word for it: 'Mishandling'. They avoid the legal overtones of 'assault' and the moral outrage and violation implicit in 'abuse'. Neglect, cruelty, non-accidental injury, sexual interference are all called 'mishandling'. All of these problems are filtered through specialized Confidential Doctor bureaux, which are a network of agencies throughout the country run by well-known paediatricians. They implicitly and explicitly set the guidelines about the way children should be treated. Their aim is to make sure the children are properly 'handled', within their own family. They are not interested in prosecuting or punishing a guilty parent. They see the law as a useful tool, not a solution. They want every parent to understand that children have an absolute right to a normal physical and emotional development.

The experiment began in 1972, when the government set up four Confidential Doctor bureaux. Drawing inspiration from Henry Kempe, the American paediatrician, and his 'battered-baby syndrome', they decided that the agencies should be predominantly medical, and knowledgeable in child development. There were several reasons for this. There had been some concern that doctors were not referring suspected cases of child abuse for fear of breaching their confidentiality. Social workers had also found it worrying that neighbours, friends and family members were hesitant to report because they wanted to remain anonymous, and feared exposure. It was also felt that consultant doctors would be given medical and psychological files and data which might be denied to other professions. Paediatricians were put in charge and given a staff of social workers and administrators to deal primarily with physical abuse.

Fifteen years later, there are ten bureaux, which cover the whole of the Netherlands. Each of them is run by two part-time doctors, supported by two or three social workers, and two or three administrators. Someone is on call twenty-four hours a day, seven days a week. Physical abuse is now only one part of their referrals. Increasingly they are burdened with the problem of sexual abuse.

Children are mainly referred by neighbours or friends, but can be reported by the families themselves, by hospital doctors and by the general practitioners. The Confidential Doctor service is well publicized.

Once a case has been reported the doctor and social workers immediately find out about the family and try to discover what help they might need. The doctor uses his medical network, and the social workers use their community contacts to find out, discreetly, as much as possible, before approaching the family.

If the bureau staff suspect that there is some 'mishandling', they will arrange for the child to come to the bureau with a friendly adult. The doctor will talk to the child about what has been happening at home, listen to his or her story, and then make contact with the parents. If the problem is serious the parents will be asked to come to the office as soon as possible and the child may well be kept away from home until they arrive. The bureau staff have no obligation to inform the police, but they might let them know what is happening. Liaison with the police is friendly and regular. Some police stations actually have social workers on their staff specifically to handle child-abuse cases. The police defer to the Confidential Doctor about possible investigations. Prosecutions are seen as a last resort.

When the parents come to the bureau there will be a discussion about the 'mishandling' and the doctor or his social workers will try to make them accept responsibility for what they have done and agree some programme. They will argue that they are pursuing the best course of action for the child and will try to convince the parents to co-operate. The Confidential Doctor carries a great deal of authority and is well respected, so his recommendations are difficult to resist. This process is considered crucial. Once the parents accept responsibility for what they have done, they can begin to understand how they are infringing the rights of their child. The children may need protection, but they also need parental support. Without that, the paediatricians feel, the child has little hope of improving.

Most parents co-operate. If they do not, and the abuse is serious, the Confidential Doctor will threaten to report them to the police or the Child Protection Board, which investigates for the courts. Normally this threat is used as a lever to make parents accept responsibility in their family. The child might be sent to the police station to talk to an investigating officer and see if there is a case worth prosecuting, even though no allegations are lodged or any formal statement made. This might be quite informal. But if the parents deny everything and refuse to co-operate, the Confidential Doctor will inform the Child Protection Board and give them enough evidence to start proceedings. When all else fails, the law takes over.

We went to Holland to meet the two Confidential Doctors in Amsterdam. Both work part-time and have a permanent staff of three social workers to handle the $3\frac{1}{2}$ million people in their catchment area. Dr Arend Koers is a well-respected consultant paediatrician in a large Amsterdam hospital. Dr Cees De Waal, his paediatric colleague, runs a medical day-care centre for children with behavioural or medical problems. They work in a converted town house on the south side of Amsterdam. There is one large open-plan office and three whitewashed consulting rooms. The phone never stops ringing. Last year they had 1,150 new reports to follow, check out and supervise. All the staff receive calls and deal with them equally. The more difficult cases of sexual abuse tend to be taken by the Confidential Doctors themselves when they are in the office. They have five new referrals each day. Once a week they hold a meeting and discuss cases. They have no explicit guidelines, but the social workers clearly defer constantly to the doctors. The social workers we met had specialized in child abuse but claimed that they pick up most of their working knowledge from the doctors themselves.

Dr De Waal explained their ideas: 'There are two ways of dealing with children who have been mishandled by their parents. One is to take them out of their families, what we in Holland call the old-fashioned way, and prevent them from being further mishandled by their parents. But often when the children go to

institutions they are further abused. The worst stories I get now
are from parents who were in institutions thirty years ago, so
that doesn't help. The other way is to try and help the family
and that is our philosophy: to try to keep the family together,
help them cope with their problems better than they did. There
is nearly always a black sheep – one of the children took the
blame for everything that was wrong. If you can change the
mechanism which produces that, then there is a chance of
stopping the mishandling. If a child is young enough it will
change immediately. If it is older it will require more time
and careful handling. It is not easy. You need many different
agencies. We the doctors cannot do it; we can only advise. We
may need therapists, we may need special schools. You cannot
simply say to people, "Stop mishandling. Stop child abuse." For
most families it is a way of communicating.'

The Confidential Doctors do not treat the cases themselves,
but will suggest a programme they consider appropriate. They
think of themselves as 'activators', putting families in touch
with other agencies or professionals. There is no general social
services department as in Britain, but there is a myriad of small
voluntary agencies, self-help groups and therapists to choose
from. The Confidential Doctor will consult with the social
workers and make recommendations. There might be a decision
to send the father to an Alcoholics Anonymous group, the
mother to a child-care and therapy course and the child to
some intensive treatment. Once the plan is activated, the social
workers at the bureau co-ordinate and supervise the programme.
They never treat anyone themselves.

Even in cases of sexual abuse, prosecution is seen as a last
resort. Dr De Waal explained: 'In order to punish, you have to
be able to prove there has been some mishandling – a neighbour
has to have seen it, someone has to testify and they have to
testify about one or two incidents on some particular day at a
definite time. The father can say, "I just lost my temper on that
particular day." So you cannot prove anything. You can only
prove those dramatic cases that are in the newspapers. That is
one end of the spectrum. Obviously I feel as strongly about rape
and extreme violence as you do, but that is only the tip of the
iceberg. The bulk of the problem cannot be solved by law:
what's happening there is not serious enough to put someone

in prison. If you bring children up with a set of standards which are inappropriate for a healthy development and not fit for having a normal family life afterwards then you are mishandling your child. But this is not about one or two isolated incidents, it is about a pattern of behaviour.'

The bureau's aim is to help the families who have serious problems and who know things are wrong, but who are unable to put things right themselves. The extreme cases of violence or rape will always go on trial. The bureau staff are far more concerned with catching those who have not yet developed a criminal pattern, and the way to do that, they feel, is if their service is seen as helping and non-punitive. Then they can work on the whole family instead of isolating one guilty one.

'The classical mishandling family', explained Dr De Waal, 'is isolated from its neighbours, isolated from its family and we do not know how to penetrate those families and change patterns.' Their anxiety is that the longer they leave the mishandling families, the more serious the abuse. The earlier they spot them and the younger the children, the better their chance of avoiding the extreme excesses of abuse. So the bureaux are designed to encourage everyone to seek support and help in complete confidence without the threat of punishment. Their hope is that if they diagnose and cure correctly, they will prevent excessive mishandling.

Dr Koers, the Confidential Doctor, compares their approach to that followed in Britain: 'In England, people I have spoken to spend a great deal of time treating the victims and families of offenders, particuarly in sexual abuse, after they have gone to prison. We are not interested in that. For us that is the smallest part of the problem. We are not interested in making people feel guilty or punishing. We want to treat families and people so that they can live together and not go to prison.'

The bureaux spread their net wide to try and catch the mishandlers. When they first started, in 1972, the Confidential Doctors were preoccupied with physical abuse. Since 1978 they have widened their scope enormously. They now have eight different types of 'mishandling' which they hope to identify and change.

*Physical* – where children are beaten, kicked, bruised, violently shaken, burned, etc.

*Neglect* – where children are dirty, unkempt, ill-fed or poorly fed without a properly balanced diet; families who do not keep doctors' appointments, who do not send their children to school.

*Emotional* – where parents ask the child to perform impossible tasks, to perform very well at school, to look after younger children; where parents shout at the child, where children are failing to thrive for some non-organic reason. The bureaux consider health-clinic check-ups absolutely essential in this category, especially for babies who cannot talk.

*Isolation* – emotional neglect where parents fail to give the child the proper love, warmth and attention that he or she needs to develop properly, where he or she is cut off from neighbours and larger family. Some parents are incapable of giving any love, so it is important to pick up those signs.

*Cognitive neglect* – where children are encouraged not to attend school, where parents are jealous that a child is learning too much, or learning different things from them (like sex education). If parents are generally negative about school, refusing to attend meetings, never seeing the teacher for an appointment, the teacher might inform the Confidential Doctor, who will talk to them himself. He in turn will probably refer them back to a teacher. Most often this concerns parents who are psychotic themselves and present the child with a bizarre view of reality. If, as Dr De Waal explained, 'you grow up in a family where you are told that you can never go upstairs if the moon is full, you get the wrong set of standards later on. If the parents are not treatable then we have to wait for symptoms in the child which gives us the right to intervene even if the parents say that they don't want us to. Sometimes you can see the child is not making normal contacts. So at that stage you might approach the parents and explain that their child is having some difficulty at school and is becoming increasingly isolated because he is frightened of going upstairs. We will explain to the parents that we realize they believe that too, but point out that this needs to change for the sake of the child. There are, of course, parents who cannot change, and then we have to think of taking the child away.'

*Institutional mishandling* – where the teacher beats the children at the school or is too busy to be concerned properly with them; where staff in children's homes are stretched and overworked and are not giving the children proper attention, or are punishing them too heavily, like keeping them in solitary confinement for too long.

*Sexual mishandling* – this is the largest category of referrals to the Confidential Doctors, comprising about one-third of their case-load. This type of mishandling occurs mainly between father and daughter, and typically the daughter will report it when she is fourteen or fifteen and has her first boyfriend. In most cases her sexual mishandling will have been going on for some years and the effects are very difficult to treat. The most difficult victims are those who have been both physically and sexually abused at the same time.

*Sexual neglect* – parents who speak unfavourably of their bodies, who refuse to talk about sexual development, who are derogatory about the child's body. Sometimes the school will pick this up and the Confidential Doctor will try to find someone for the child to talk to – a schoolteacher, family member or neighbour. The doctor will also ask the schoolteachers if they can talk it over with the parents.

Some of those categories are familiar everywhere. Others, like cognitive and sexual neglect, emotional neglect and isolation would be quite strange to anyone in England. Initially they smack of the nanny state, a concept thoroughly alien to most of us who jealously guard parental rights. But the Dutch Confidential Doctors are quick to point out that this list of eight areas does not mean there is an ideal way to bring up children, or that anyone who displays any one form of this neglect is a 'mishandler'. It is simply a way of identifying the varieties of neglect. It does not mean that everyone should or even could bring up their children in blissful harmony, and that every family has to be happy. It does mean that there are certain warning signs which may give cause for concern and a reason for intervening. There is a clear-cut expectation and a set of standards implicit in all of this which might worry the English social worker.

Dr Koers takes the definition further and considers that 'mishandling' is both active and passive. Besides physical and sexual violence, there are the omissions which can be equally violent for a growing child. The mother who does nothing and takes no responsibility for the care and development of her child is as culpable as the parent who is physically violent. Both are abrogating their parental responsibility. Koers has no absolute standard of parenthood, but he does have an absolute standard of what a healthy and growing child should be like.

All the children who come under Koers's care are measured in two different ways. One is purely physical – height and weight as in the percentile chart. The other is a behavioural and emotional development chart which again has an average curve. If the child falls markedly above or below that curve, Koers investigates further. For example, when a child goes into hospital for some treatment he or she will regress after a day, and will then pick up and become his or her normal self. If a child takes longer to regress than he or she should, and longer to return to his or her normal self, then warning bells will ring.

Koers's chart is quite complex. He and his team will observe a child, make a number of inquiries about him or her and collect enough information to score his or her behaviour under a series of very distinct headings. He needs to know how the child behaves with his or her peers; whether the child is friendly, aggressive or affectionate; how the child relates to his or her parents; whether the child is docile, passive, physical, etc.; how the child behaves and plays on his or her own, and whether with his or her brothers or sisters, or with other adults; whether the child's behaviour is extrovert, aggressive, hyperactive, inattentive; how much attachment and physical contact he or she displays and how much deprivation. From all of this Koers produces an index which he will compare to the index of a normal child of that age. He can then tell immediately whether anything is wrong, and whether to intervene.

Interestingly this is not a set of guidelines which his colleague uses. Dr De Waal places a great deal of emphasis on behaviour patterns, as well as on simple medical information. He runs a medical day-care centre attended by children who have medical symptoms like continuous headaches, asthma, pulling out their hair, hyperactivity and so on. They are all living at home, but attend the centre every day, often with their parents. The centre is staffed by speech therapists, psychologists, physiotherapists and teachers. He notes, 'Once you start treating those children with the parents you always see that a large proportion of the families have developed a way of communicating with each other that will ultimately lead to abuse unless it is changed. And in those cases you see very clearly the effect of re-educating the parents. Very often those parents have themselves been badly abused when they were children. Everyone knows that the symptoms of the children come from the interactions within the family. At the centre we give the children proper care and attention and develop their interests and concentration. At the same time the social workers work with the parents. We never use a heavy term like mishandling. It is all done very subtly, but the mechanism for working with that is exactly the same as working in the Confidential Doctor bureaux with the problems of abuse and mishandling. You can see very quickly that once the children begin to change their behaviour, so the parents tend to change as well.'

De Waal considers that the parents nearly always want to change. They want to be good parents, but they simply do not know how. 'They all say,' he told us sadly, "I want to do right for my kids. I want them to have it better than me." That's where child abuse starts. If you don't intervene, nothing will happen and the child will become more and more difficult and it will end in some form of violence.' So he sees violence as forming part of a continuum which needs to be avoided. In that sense he is looking for and picking up the same signs as his colleague with his sophisticated chart. But neither of them has guidelines and procedures, both rely on their long experience and their understanding of the nature of abuse.

Despite the many guidelines and booklets thrust at the British social worker, a great deal of the important decisions are subjective, based on assessment of the clients and their attitudes. The Confidential Doctors never get personally involved in the clients. Their role is to diagnose and to suggest and supervise treatments or cures. They may not have guidelines, but they certainly have explicit standards about the developing child which embrace behavioural abnormalities as well as physical symptoms like bruises and burns.

No concessions are made to different ethnic groups like Turks or Moroccans working in the Netherlands. In Britain it is accepted that West Indians sometimes 'overchastise' their children. The Dutch make no such exceptions. 'At the beginning,' recalls De Waal, 'we thought that perhaps they had different ways of bringing up their children and we had to let them know that we cannot accept any child being bruised or wounded here.' They are quite happy to accept the cultural differences providing it does not affect the acceptable physical and emotional development of the children. Dr Koers told us firmly: 'These people are now living in a Dutch system. They cannot behave as if they were in a Moroccan desert. Their children are going to grow up here and so the parents have to understand what is acceptable for normal children here. Here we allow our girls to go out and meet naturally with boys. We do not believe that wounding a child to make him obey is good or useful. So we have to try and change their ways.'

Trying to bring about changes in the immigrant population is not easy. The families may be approached through someone respected in their community or through their church.

'But', notes Dr De Waal, 'there you have a real problem. If stress is one of the reasons why child abuse takes place then an immigrant population will have far more stresses than people in their own country, in their own familiar background. Homesickness and cultural clashes cause even greater problems. So it is very difficult to treat.'

Both the Confidential Doctors agree that co-operation with the parents is crucial if they want to help the child. They cannot make any changes if the child and the parents do not want them. If they receive a report on a girl who is having sexual relations with her father and both her parents deny that it is happening and she herself does not want it to stop, there is nothing they can do except threaten legal intervention. It will then fall upon the shoulders of the Child Protection Board to investigate and the judge to make a decision. The Confidential Doctor will not become involved as a witness. At this point the case is out of his hands. But they assure us this very rarely happens.

While we were at the bureau, a young girl came in to see Dr Koers. Annalise Visser was a slender, blonde fourteen-year-old. She had phoned previously to make an appointment and had arrived early. She told him that for the last four years her mother's brother had been having sex with her and she wanted it to stop. Koers was convinced that what she told him was true, not simply because of the way she told the story, but because of her current problems. Koers discovered in a brief interview that she had difficulties making contact with boys of her own age, she had recurrent nightmares, she was doing poorly at school and had bad reports, she tended to quarrel with her teachers about nothing, and she constantly had the feeling that everyone was blaming her for everything. 'All these signs make me sure', he told us, 'that she is a victim of sexual abuse.'

Koers asked the girl what she wanted to do, and she told him that above all she hoped to see her uncle punished. He discussed this with her and told her that there might be better ways of dealing with the problem and keeping her safe. Annalise had thought only of punishment and ridding herself of the menace. The Confidential Doctor's solution was slightly different. His plan was to talk to her parents in the office and to discuss the problem in front of Annalise. He would then talk to the uncle, and make him understand what he had done. Annalise accepted his solution.

Koers phoned the parents immediately; they were extremely angry and wanted to go straight to the police. Koers told them they could do that if they wanted to but it would mean a long wait during which nothing would be accomplished and everyone would become even more anxious. He suggested instead that they visit him. He put it rather more formally: 'As the Confidential Doctor I invite you to come to my office to talk over with you what has happened and what is best to do for your daughter.' The parents decided to take up the offer.

Next, Koers will 'invite' the uncle to the bureau and explain 'What your niece has told me about what you have done to her I believe is true. I can see the effects and consequences of all of this in her behaviour. She is having a very difficult time with her friends and at school because of the predicament in which you have placed her. It will become even more difficult. All this is your responsibility. She is not the guilty one, you are.' Then, Koers told us, 'I will make him take the responsibility for what he has done, and see the troubles he has caused and I will make him face the girl and her parents.'

If the uncle refuses to accept the responsibility for what he has done, and will not talk to the girl or her parents, Koers's solution is simple: 'I say, "Okay, I cannot force you to do anything or to come to the office to see me, or to talk to the girl. But if you don't do this I will advise the parents to go to the police, and then they can follow it up in their way."' The uncle will be aware that the Confidential Doctor himself will give a report to the Child Protection Board. He will also know that Annalise will be seeing a therapist who will likewise hand in a report. His options are clear. Koers has no doubt which he will choose. Ninety per cent of his cases accept his recommendations, accept their responsibility and submit to treatment.

This 'confrontational method' is used by Koers in all his cases of sexual abuse. They follow a set pattern. The child first tells the sad tale to someone he or she trusts – a friend, a teacher, a neighbour. That person in turn tells the Confidential Doctor. He in turn will invite the child to his bureau and assess the case. If he believes the child's story he will then invite the mother to attend. He will arrange a meeting with the child present and explain what has been happening. If the mother does not accept it, he will make the child repeat the story for the mother.

The reaction of the mother is crucial, particularly if the father is the perpetrator. Koers explains: 'We have to know whether the mother is accusing the daughter, saying it is all her fault, or whether she is taking her part. If the mother takes the father's part against the daughter, because she is afraid of losing her husband, then we, the Confidential Doctor, must become the advocate for the child. The child needs protection and therapy. If the parents will not co-operate then we must go to the Child Protection Board and suggest the child should be taken away. If the mother co-operates and is sympathetic to the daughter then we do not need to take the child away, although it may be necessary for the father to go. But the girl must have the support of the mother.' He feels that without the co-operation of the mother the child has no one to support her in the family against the father. If the mother cannot be made to understand, the child has no way of finding her own identity in that family.

Next in the sequence, the Confidential Doctor will invite the perpetrator, usually the father, and the child to his office. He will explain to the father the damage he has caused, how he has interfered with his daughter's development, the short- and long-term consequences of his actions and will emphasize that it is entirely his responsibility. Acting on behalf of the child, Koers will argue forcibly that no child is at fault in these circumstances. The adult cannot excuse his actions or rationalize them. He has misused his power and damaged the child. He has to face up to that, accept responsibility for what he has done and make it clear to the child that it is he who is guilty, not her.

After that, if the father accepts the argument and decides to co-operate the Confidential Doctor will arrange a family meeting to discuss the best programme of action. They may need individual therapy, or they may need therapy together. 'Before you treat the daughter you nearly always have to treat the mother, as she tends to be jealous of the attention lavished on the daughter and will nearly always have severe problems of her own. We first have to look into the backgrounds of the parents and we invariably find that they themselves have had some sort of abuse which they are perpetuating in their own family. So we have to treat the mother's own triangle; that is, her relationship with her own two parents in which perhaps she herself was a victim, and then the father's own triangle, before we can begin to start on the triangle that involves the current crisis. For that you need time. It may take two or three years; it could take nine or ten.'

The history of the parents, Koers feels, is central to unravelling the problem. The cycle repeats relentlessly between one generation and another. Dr De Waal told us: 'I have never come across a family in which child abuse took place in whatever form where there was nothing wrong with the personal history of the parents, and when I say wrong, I mean something badly wrong with their own family or upbringing.'

The role of the Confidential Doctor once some programme has been agreed is supervisory. The system of treatment and support is far more flexible than that in England and the doctors can work out a variety of treatment patterns and change them if they prove ineffective. But they do have difficulty, as their colleagues do in Britain, in finding therapists and psychiatrists willing to invest a great deal of time in this type of case.

The treatment depends on the age of the child and on the family conditions. The close working relationship with the police gives the doctors some leverage with the parents. But they have no power to take a child away from home unless the child wants it. That must be referred to the Child Protection Board, and then in turn to a judge. De Waal complained that he had many files of children where he had recommended that the child be taken away but the courts had ruled otherwise. So the doctors' authority is limited in this way by law. But they still have an advantage over the social workers working in Britain or the USA through their access to confidential material on the child.

Taking the child away is always the last resort. De Waal assured us: 'I try to use that option as rarely as possible. Both I and the Child Protection Board firmly believe that the best interest of the child is to remain in his own family.' So they are as keen as we are to keep the child in the family. 'We have a distinct advantage as Confidential Doctors when we testify to the Child Protection Board. We can amass a great deal of information about that child which is not readily available to others, and because we are highly experienced in this work we bring to it a great deal more experience than a doctor who might only testify perhaps four or five times in his career.'

The Confidential Doctors rarely appear in court. They give their evidence to the Child Protection Board which in turn will use their statements as part of the court evidence. Children too are spared appearances in court by interviews with the Child Protection Board. This also avoids the long delay in waiting for cases to appear.

When we explained to De Waal that children in Britain could wait up to nine months for a court hearing and during that time receive no treatment he was astonished. 'But that's ridiculous,' he exclaimed. 'That's child abuse. It shows that society is not able to handle the problem. It may be correct in a legal sense but the child is a victim and above all she needs treatment. She certainly does not need a system where for nine months she is put in a vacuum waiting for the court to grind into action. Our legal system is similar. You might find plenty of arguments against the Confidential Doctor but we do have a certain status and we use that quite unashamedly to influence judges and magistrates into making faster decisions and avoiding delays when we think that is necessary.'

The object of the Confidential Doctors is to keep everyone but those who are extremely violent or completely un-cooperative out of the legal system, and to keep the family to-gether. 'The last thing the child wants,' claimed De Waal, 'except in extreme cases, is for the father to leave. If society thinks they know better then victims will keep their mouth shut.' He believes that even in cases of sexual abuse it is preferable to keep the family together. He feels this method is successful and quotes cases where the family have faced up to what they have done, and so are unlikely to reoffend if the family dynamics have changed. De Waal explained, 'One of the main things which must happen in a family where sexual abuse has taken place is that the loyalty between the two sex partners must be restored. If the mother is made aware of what happened and it is impossible for her to continue to deny it and she is made aware of her responsibility for her daughter, then very often it stops. Most fathers aren't sex maniacs, they have enormous feelings of guilt. But the longer you wait, the more difficult it is to change. That is why we want to make it possible for people to tell us about it early. Then we can check the risk factors.'

In Britain it would be most unusual for the police not to be informed, particularly in cases of sexual abuse. They would also be likely to attend the first case conference and take part in a discussion about whether to prosecute. But the decision to prosecute rests with the police, and they will be far more likely to take the matter to court than their Dutch colleagues. A study by R. J. Christopherson that compared the two methods in 1976 found: 'Of 109 Case Conferences in one English area, police action of some sort was taken in 25 cases out of the 53 in which a child was found to be injured. In the Netherlands, on the other hand, of the 899 cases in 1976 only 30 were reported to the public prosecutor with a view to criminal proceedings.'

Both Dr De Waal and Dr Koers are convinced that the child wants the mishandling or abuse to stop but does not want to lose his or her family. Simply pointing an accusing finger at the perpetrator will not help the child. The family as a whole is involved. Those who see and do nothing are as responsible as those who actually mishandle. So the dynamics of the family has to be altered.

Both doctors agree that if a child has been sexually abused from an early age he or she will be very difficult to treat, particularly during his or her early teens. But that in no way deters them. Koers quoted the late Dr Kempe, who received a call one evening from a therapist who did not know how to handle a client. 'Well,' replied Dr Kempe, 'if you do not know what to do, then you need to know more.' 'And that', comments Koers, 'is our attitude. If we don't know how to help we shouldn't blame the parents but ourselves for not knowing more.'

It is difficult to gauge the success of the Dutch doctors' methods. There are no reoffending rates since so few are prosecuted anyway. Once the doctors have plugged their clients into a set of programmes their involvement is minimal except in a co-ordinating and supervisory role, so they tend to lose touch. They are both quite sure their method works, although some families might have recurrent problems and it might take a very long time to treat them successfully.

If all else fails families are offered support and shelter in a safe house. There are two of these in Holland and the one in Amsterdam is called Der Triangel. Perched on the banks of a canal, this traditional five-floor seventeenth-century house takes in the toughest multi-problem families in the country. Yet the mood of the staff is buoyant. Most of the families who arrive on their doorstep are so hopeless that almost any change seems a miracle.

Families are referred there mostly by the Confidential Doctor. Some apply voluntarily, and some are sent there to work out suspended prison sentences. Most of the families are what they call 'proto professionalized': they have been dealing with the various welfare organizations for years, and are still incapable of organizing their lives. Many of them have every sort of problem. They might be drug addicts or alcoholics, be in debt, have prison records; and they might have grossly mishandled their children in several ways. Nearly all have some incest problem along with everything else. They are allowed six months in the house and then they have to leave. There is an elaborate after-care service which may operate for anything up to five years afterwards.

In the house families live together in groups. There are four groups, and three families in each group. Each member of the family will have his or her own bedroom and they will share a communal living room and bathroom with the rest of their group. No one cooks – they are given food in the large cafeteria, and everyone eats together. The families have to keep their part of the house clean, and have to work out routines and rotas and look after their own children. There is an enormous staff to help them. We counted about seventy-five people attached to the house, although many of those were on shift work. But there is a doctor, three psychologists, one psychiatrist, a number of social workers, child-care workers and welfare workers plus all the administrative, cooking and cleaning staff. The Dutch government picks up the bill.

The stay is designed to make the parents more responsible. 'Responsible' is a word that occurs constantly. Mr Gertlam Lind, one of the directors, told us: 'We do not take the view that one of them is guilty, even if they are the one who has badly mishandled their child, has wounded him or has had incest. We think that both parents are guilty, although we never use the word guilty. We feel they are both responsible. For whatever happens is a result of the parents' relationship to each other as much as their relationship to the children. The mother may not have actually had incest, but she might have chosen to ignore it because of her own failings. When women claim they do not know what went on, we do not believe them. And mostly we are right. It may be that she herself was an incest victim and chose a particularly vulnerable man who cannot support her and she in a way deliberately offers him the child as a way of drawing him into her own problems. The man may well then do the mishandling, but it is useless to make him feel guilty. If either continues to just feel guilty and nothing more you never get any sort of working alliance. Both the parents have to realize what they are doing if there is any hope that the family will stay together.'

Most of the guilt, which they all discuss at length, is due to their own upbringing, the Triangel workers find. The parents themselves have suffered terribly at the hands of their own parents and have never really thought about that. They have only reacted against it angrily. So the staff try to remind parents of their own childhood. As Lind told us, 'We try to strip the adult down to a child again so that we can begin to build a better adult.' And to do this they have endless 'talks' or therapy. No one likes the term 'therapy', and the staff have learned not to use it with the families as it tends to put them off. If one of the mothers is too depressed to get out of bed, someone may bring her a cup of tea and talk with her and comfort her. If a parent shouts belligerently at a child over a meal or lashes out at a child there will be a 'talk'. There are also regular 'talks' with the psychologists and workers.

The routine in the house is fairly structured. All the families breakfast together and then they take their children to school. For many of the children it is the first time they have attended school regularly. The parents are then talked to either separately or together. They are encouraged to take up some activity so that they do not sit around the house all day. They might do a course in carpentry or sewing, or take up swimming or decorating. At midday, all the children return briefly for lunch. The parents are looked after by the group workers until the children finish school at 4 p.m. Then the parents are encouraged to play with the children and the workers. All this time suggestions are slowly made about why the child is kicking or fighting and what might engage him or her more successfully. Gradually the parents learn to play with them. The workers at the house often find at first that the parents want to play themselves, since they have never done that before and are jealous of letting their children play.

Meal times are very intense and one disruptive family can cause all the other children to get distressed or play up and yell. So if any of the workers notice the tension building up in one family, they and others in the group will try to defuse it. If for example a mother gets more and more exasperated because none of her children will eat the vegetables, she may start shouting at them. Someone will immediately intervene and calmly start talking about the food to the mother or the children, or distract the child so that the mother can calm down. At all times the workers try to get the parents to encourage the positive sides of their children and minimize the negative sides. And the staff do the same to the parents.

One of the ways they encourage the parents to gain confidence in themselves is through massage. They find that women who are overweight, who do not have good standards of personal hygiene and who are generally unkempt tend to develop a new sense of themselves through massage. Most of these women have themselves never been loved or cared for, and the massage gives them for the first time a sense of their own bodies and a pleasure in their bodies. Physiotherapists find that after a course of massage the women will begin to take much greater care of themselves. They will dress cleanly, make sure their hair is attractive and even start wearing make-up. The staff at the Triangel are conscious of not doing anything too intensively, as they feel that 'could disintegrate a person who anyway has so little personal resources'.

Once the children are in bed, at about 9 or 10 p.m. the families in the group will sit around and chat. The atmosphere is remarkably peaceful and quiet, except when the occasional child wakes up. Lind explained why: 'Most of the families we get have always been quite isolated. They have never made friends or any close contacts at all, so this is quite a new experience for them. They have also tended to blame the outside world for all their troubles and their isolation without realizing that they too are partly responsible. If they talk about this to families who have had similar emotional experiences, they realize that things don't just happen to you, you can make things happen yourself and change.'

All the support and treatment is given to make sure the parents can continue to look after the children. If the workers find that the handling of the children is not improving, then the treatment like massage may stop and a new technique begun.

Sometimes after a stay at the Triangel parents decide to separate. But that is not seen as a failure. If the adults have gained some confidence and feel they can manage alone and examine their feelings constructively, they have learned to work out something for themselves. The staff think they have failed if the parents are still just as incapable of looking after the children as they were when they came in. But that, they told us, is rare.

No physical violence is allowed in the house. If tempers flare and it ends in a fight or a beating, families are asked to leave, and the other families are extremely critical. But Lind comments, with extraordinary tolerance: 'If a beating starts then we must have done something wrong. After all an act like that is the result of tension building up over some time. We should have been aware of that – perhaps then we could have avoided it.'

No one appears to know how successful the method is. The

workers point out that the families they receive are really at the end of the line, quite incapable of looking after themselves or their children, so it is not easy to compare them to normal families. The staff are teaching people to shop and account for money, who previously were unable to housekeep. They are making people aware of personal cleanliness for the first time, teaching them how to iron, to play with and talk to their children. Some of the families did not even realize when they first came in that you had to put extra clothes on the children when the weather got colder. They are what the English social workers describe in their own curious jargon as 'extremely low in parenting skills'.

The Van Haaren family was fairly typical of the multiple problems the Triangel faces. The parents had been given suspended prison sentences because their two-year-old had died of neglect. Instead of serving a term in prison they were sent to the Triangel. There were three other children, all under five. The eldest child was what they called parentified. At four and a half she had taken over many of the mother's jobs before they came to the Triangel. She went shopping, she dressed the younger children, she made meals, she tied the children's shoelaces and so on. But because she was so young she did not do any of those things properly, so the parents were continuously angry with her. The father was a long-distance lorry driver, away a great deal of the time. The mother spent most of her evenings in bars with a variety of men. They lived in a small town where they were quite cut off from their extended family. The man's parents would have nothing to do with them as they did not like the daughter-in-law. Her parents would have nothing to do with them because she had been sexually involved with her own father. He had continued the incest even after she had been married. In fact there was some suspicion that one of the children was her own father's.

At the beginning of their stay none of the children would play alone or speak without their brothers and sisters present. They were quite unable to make friends or relate in any way to other children or other adults. The eldest parent child was very serious and never played. She watched her parents and her sisters constantly. The parents had no idea how to play with the children. None of the family could operate at all if separate from each other. They had been ostracized by their neighbours after the death of their child and were tormented by guilt and by the feeling that the whole world was against them.

After six months at the Triangel, the staff report that the eldest girl, who has had a great deal of play therapy, can now play on her own quite happily, and is talking properly. All the children can now make friends and do not need to exist in a defensive family huddle. The parents have actually begun to play with their children and sit on the floor with toys, bricks and paintings. Initially the children had not dared to disobey their parents at all and watched them unwaveringly. After a few months they began to rebel slightly and constantly say no. That caused problems for the parents, who were used to unquestioned obedience. Gradually they were shown how to adapt and understand why the children were saying no. They now allow them some freedom of expression.

They also began to make contact with other families in the house. The mother had only had casual men acquaintances besides her husband. He himself had no friends because he was always away. They had rowed constantly and he had drunk heavily. They had never talked about their dead child. But after a few months of 'talking' at the Triangel, they both went to visit his grave. They also began to talk to each other. Most importantly, after a few months the father finally arranged to see his own family and take the children with him; and the wife managed to win through her anger and pain and talk to her father about their incest.

The wife had been given a great deal of massage. Lind explained to us: 'Incest works very strongly on bodily feelings. People feel dirty, ugly, used. Massage helps them to like their bodies and be aware of themselves. But we have to be careful not to disrupt her too much. She has so few feelings of her own and they have to be built gradually.'

The family will eventually have to leave the womb-like support of the Triangel and try to manage on their own. The staff feel optimistic about their chances. They are hopeful that now that they have learned about household finances they will not fall into debt immediately. They feel sure that the fortnightly meetings and talks in after-care will reinforce the work that has already begun. They feel the children have a chance now of building some life for themselves separate from the relentless demands of their parents. Judging success with this family is quite difficult. If, of course, another child is severely neglected, the Triangel has failed abjectly. But, given the long-term supportive after-care service, the staff feel that is unlikely.

They do not measure success, although presumably the children could be checked, in the same way that Dr Koers measures all his patients. It costs £45 a day to keep each person in the house, which is about one-quarter of the cost of hospital. They clear up a large number of the families' financial difficulties and teach them how to look after themselves so that when they leave they are much less of a drain on the welfare services. The true investment, they would claim, is in the next generation. If the abusing parents inflict their own stunted and crippled upbringing on their children, yet another generation of future abusers is let loose. If this treatment can break the vicious cycle then the saving to society is enormous.

Almost every social services department in Britain has several key, well-known problem families who have been on the books for years and who spawn endless problems. They take up the most time and dominate the social worker's case-load. There are three solutions to this dilemma: all their children can be removed; the family can be shored up with as much practical help as possible; or the parents can be made to change.

Der Triangel is a stab at changing the impossible. Judging from the waiting list, which often numbers over twenty families, there is some belief that this can be done. To many outside Holland the Triangel solution can be seen to be on the one hand more intrusive and on the other more liberal. By defining 'mishandling' in such a broad way they move into areas which would be considered anathema to the British public who would like to see the state as far removed from their private lives as possible. Cognitive neglect and sexual neglect would be received with some disbelief.

The Dutch are far less punitive in these matters and more tolerant of people's difficulties than the British. The supporters of law and order would receive fairly short shrift in Holland. The Dutch are loath to involve the law, wary about sending people to jail, and insistent on keeping families together. The Confidential Doctor system tries seriously to represent the child in an adult world. The doctors do not nod in the direction of parents' inalienable rights. The child is firmly centre-stage. But because they are always looking for the best solution for the child, they often take what others might consider considerable risks with problem families. Most striking of all, the Dutch government is willing to invest in ways of breaking the generation cycle.

The status and authority of the Confidential Doctors contribute in no small measure to the way the whole problem of mishandling is seen. The paediatricians who run the bureax have a great deal of political influence and are well respected in legal circles. They also command the respect of the police and the public and so have the space to write their own charter for the child and his or her development. There are inevitable checks and balances, through the auspices of the courts, and through financial restrictions. As child specialists in a unique role, the Confidential Doctors influence the treatment of children and shape public opinion.

They are not content with dealing with the families only after they have produced problem children. Dr De Waal sees the need for a massive education programme to catch people even before they enter the orbit of the Confidential Doctor. 'People need more information about what it means to bring up children, what children need if they are difficult. It might be an enormous help in preventing child abuse. You often see that a child who kicks his parents will kick his friends and his teachers at the day-care centre and everyone thinks "Hey, you little stinker, why are you kicking me?" instead of asking the question, "What is he trying to say by kicking me?" And that's how the children begin to show their problems. If you can make parents aware of that you might be able to break the circle. If you ignore it or simply punish it, then you are beginning the path towards abuse. The only thing that can break the cycle is more knowledge and more understanding about how to bring up children, and about what children need. There are plenty of people around who have that knowledge and understanding, paediatricians, psychologists, educationalists. But it rarely reaches the people it needs to.'

Dr De Waal's colleague Dr Koers is at pains to point out that they are concerned fundamentally with the physical and emotional development of the child. There are many patterns of parental behaviour he personally does not like, but only if and when it appears to damage or is likely to affect the child's development would he interfere. His primary guideline is that the well-being of the child is the overriding priority: the child must always be put first.

# 10 'IT SHOULDN'T HURT
##        TO BE A CHILD'

Many years ago Dr Henry Kempe, the American paediatrician who first identified what he called 'the battered-child syndrome', wrote,

> Child abuse is a problem but not a hopeless one. Anyone who reads about physically or emotionally abused children, or deals with them daily, must sometimes feel pessimistic about whether we will ever be able to give every child the start in life he deserves. But it is important not to underestimate the huge strides now being made. We must not be demoralized or fail to keep pushing forward.

Those words are as true as ever today. In spite of the sense of defeat and frustration caused by the apparent increase in cases of every kind of abuse, and the inability of the welfare services to prevent it recurring time and time again, there are signs that the issue is now high on the political agenda in Britain, and that growing public concern has produced more openness, more readiness to deal with those distressing aspects of domestic life which were previously hidden as shameful family secrets. The judge in the recent case of four-year-old Kimberley Carlile, kicked to death by her stepfather, referred to the 'sordid annals' of child abuse; at least, today, those annals are acknowledged and explored.

It would be unrealistic to expect that any British government could ever introduce a system which resembled the one that seems to be working well in Holland. Our decentralized social services network, together with our much more legalistic approach to what are seen as crimes against children, make it impossible to superimpose a special new structure for dealing with child abuse. Although attitudes to the problem have become less inhibited in Britain, there is no suggestion that abuse should be completely removed from the criminal justice system as it has been in Holland, except in the very last resort. Just recently the Home Secretary, when describing ways of making police investigations of sexual abuse less traumatic for the victims, said, 'Those who commit terrible crimes against children deserve to suffer harsh punishment; the anger and revulsion of society at such cases must be given expression.' And in 1985 the Sexual Offences Act raised the maximum penalty for indecent assault on a girl from five years to ten years and for attempted rape from seven years to life.

On the social services side the professional bodies who represent social workers have been ready to admit specific faults and mistakes in the wake of the official reports on child-abuse tragedies, but they are not ready to contemplate fundamental changes in the way the cases are managed. In their 1985 policy statement the British Association of Social Workers made some radical suggestions but concluded, 'In looking at the overall framework ... of child-abuse management ... the Association believes there is no viable alternative to the current structure.' Nonetheless there are important ingredients in the Dutch theory and practice which could usefully be grafted on to our systems, and there are further innovative ideas which many experts in this country are already discussing.

Perhaps the most significant development in British thinking has been the revival of the explicit emphasis on the primacy of the needs of the child in families where abuse is either suspected or known, a philosophy already well established in Holland. Since the publication of the Blom-Cooper report on the Jasmine Beckford case in 1985, every public statement from every source has insisted that the child must be given absolute priority in the management of cases where the perceived welfare of the child may conflict with the perceived happiness or wishes of the parents.

The government response to the Beckford report was that 'In any conflict of interests between the parents and the child, those of the child must always come first'; and this was echoed by the

British Association of Social Workers: 'The child is the primary client in any abusing family.' The Health Visitors Association stated: 'In the last two or three decades the health visitor's traditional child-life protection role had been replaced by concern with the whole family. This emphasis must be reviewed so that the child's interests are paramount.'

This philosophy is, of course, most important in cases where choices have to be made between fostering children who may be at risk and leaving them in their own homes, but it also comes up in many of the less obviously critical areas where customary practice has been to look at the well-being of the family as a whole rather than at the individual welfare of the child.

For example, in the case of the gross neglect of her children by Mrs Edwina Page, the professional workers several times avoided critical confrontation with Mrs Page over the children's non-attendance at medical checks or over the appalling state of their bedrooms, in order to avoid further stress to the mother. If they had considered that the children were their primary clients they might have acted differently and so have avoided the final tragedy of baby Malcolm's death.

The new and general determination that the child must be put first goes hand in hand with the growing acceptance of the view that children should have legal rights, entirely distinct from those of their parents. This is the logical conclusion of the gradual abandonment of the traditional status of children as chattels of a marriage and part of family property. Some enthusiasts have gone so far as to suggest that children should be made full citizens, with all the adult rights except the right to vote. In a country like Britain, where it is only in the last decade that it has been possible to get children adopted against the wishes of their parents, and where many courts have a clear prejudice in favour of parental wishes and parental testimony, however inadequate those parents may have proved, it seems very unlikely that such an extreme solution will be rapidly introduced. But the idea of a child's legal rights to such mundane but essential benefits as regular health checks, as well as rights to more abstract concepts like happiness and emotional fulfilment, is becoming an important influence on policy about the status of children.

The difficulties, as always, come when attempts are made to

translate the theoretical policies into the practical world of everyday welfare work. Case after case has shown that it is often almost impossible for today's social workers (who may indeed have statutory authority over children who are in care but at home) to enforce decisions against the natural authority of resident, uncooperative parents. One has only to look at the outcry of the tabloid newspapers about 'parental rights' in the case of Cleveland children being taken into care on the suspicion of sexual abuse to realize that prejudices in favour of parents as the arbiters of their children's fate run very deep. It is difficult to see how this can change very much, even if children themselves were formally to be given their own legal rights, while child abuse continues to be managed by overstretched, generalist social workers in the way that it is now. The clear evidence is that most field workers in the welfare services, who do not have specialist knowledge of the complexities of child abuse, often feel unable and unwilling to jeopardize a relationship of trust with a parent in order to assert what may be seen as a dictatorial intervention on behalf of a child.

The most notorious holder of this attitude was undoubtedly Gun Wahlstrom, the young Swedish social worker who was legally responsible for Jasmine Beckford, but who, during the last four months of the little girl's life, never even saw her. The Blom-Cooper report was uncompromising in its criticism of Gun Wahlstrom's misdirected priorities:

> Throughout the three years of social work with the Beckford family, Ms Wahlstrom totally misconceived her role as the field worker enforcing Care Orders in respect of two young children at risk. Her gaze was focused on Beverley Lorrington and Morris Beckford [the parents]; she averted her eyes from the children to be aware of them only as and when they were with their parents, hardly ever to observe their development, and never to communicate with Jasmine on her own. The two children were treated as mere appendages to their parents, who were treated as the clients.

In spite of these trenchant comments there was no suggestion that Gun Wahlstrom, or her supervisor, who was just as severely censured, were wicked or malign women. It was said that they had been grossly inadequate in monitoring the Beckford children, but that inadequacy was blamed more on their inexperience and lack of training than on personal fault.

There has been considerable debate in the last few years about reorganizing the training of social workers to give more attention to child abuse. It has been suggested that the basic training should be extended to a third year, and that field work with abusing families should be entrusted only to those who have had specific postgraduate instruction. None of these reforms has been implemented. Overall management of difficult cases can still be in the hands of young professionals, like Gun Wahlstrom, whose only instruction may have been a two-hour lecture in a very general curriculum, and who may be given a potentially lethal family to handle without any previous practical experience.

We have, therefore, to return to the basic questions about the nature of contemporary social work, which we raised in the first chapter, before we can become too sanguine about the probability of real change at the grass roots in the wake of the national-level exhortations to give the child absolute priority. It seems unlikely that any reforms in the education of social workers will really enable them to get to grips with child abuse while those workers are asked to act across the whole range of family problems. The expert opinion from Holland, and from those who have given evidence to various British inquiries, is that understanding about child abuse is only painstakingly built up over a long period, and that the subject requires undivided attention. In the debate that has so far taken place about how better to handle child abuse, there is no suggestion that there should be a return to the concept of Children's Officers, or that a new way of encouraging particular responsibilities and skills should be found. There have been demands for child-abuse 'co-ordinators' to be appointed in every area, and for more and better use of the area review committees who oversee local policy.

But, although these ideas are welcome, they tend simply to add another layer of bureaucracy to the present system rather than to improve the qualifications of the people working daily with children at risk. While they continue to be trained in the philosophy and practice of generalist social work, it is difficult to believe that they will always be able to 'put the children first', however good their intentions and however loud the public protestations that they should. If a social worker is faced by a family with a multitude of problems, like the Broadbent family in Nottingham, where violence, desertion, drunkenness, incest and neglect all have to be dealt with by the same person, it is easy to see how an ambition to give priority to the welfare of the children might be overwhelmed by a tidal wave of general crises. It seems to us that only when the system created by the Seebohm report in the early 1970s is examined in a fundamental way, so that less importance is attributed to the generalist principle of social work, can we be confident that sufficient priority will automatically be given to the needs of children at risk in families who are beset by difficulties.

One of the ways in which it is hoped to improve the management of child abuse, within the framework of the present system, is by promoting co-operation between the various welfare agencies. The most recent DHSS guidance circular is called *Working Together* and extols the necessity of collaboration between social workers, health workers and schools. Obviously if the primarily responsible social workers could call on the professional knowledge of expert colleagues, this would go a long way to alleviating anxieties about their own lack of specialism. As we have seen from the Dutch example, there is much to be said for making the medical profession the first point of reference in dealing with child abuse; doctors have the paediatric training to enable them to use the touchstones of growth and development to monitor objectively any child who may be abused. There are medical authorities in Britain, like Dr Leonard Taitz of the Sheffield Children's Hospital, who would like to see their opinions given a much more central role in the crucial decisions about where an abused child should live and who should look after him.

In the past there has been an antipathy between many social services departments and their medical counterparts, and some doctors have obscured simple procedures like weighing and measuring behind much more sophisticated data about rates of intellectual and physical development. This has meant that nearly all social workers, and even many health visitors, have protested that this kind of knowledge is beyond their understanding and outside their official remit. Recently, since the Beckford report, the need for familiarity with the basic medical tools has been impressed on all social services departments, and the need to involve local GPs and health visitors in case conferences has been underlined. At the same time, GPs have been asked to increase their involvement in child-abuse cases and, like the social workers, to pay special attention to the well-being of children in problem families.

Health visitors, who are often the front-line troops in making medical assessments of a family, since they go regularly into homes to check on small children, have also been trying to sharpen up their knowledge and their practice. The Health Visitors Association said recently: 'The HVA believes that the failure of health visitors and social workers to learn the lessons of more than twenty-five child-death inquiries demands a change in their professional response as a matter of urgency.' The most urgent but perhaps the most difficult change is for health visitors, like social workers, to assert their authority more vigorously when dealing with recalcitrant families. It should never again be possible for parents to refuse to allow their children to be weighed and measured. And, particularly if the children are in care, the health visitor should insist, through the statutory powers of the social services, that she sees the children regularly and that they have enough physical examinations to allow their development to be properly charted. The repeated problem of health visitors failing to gain access to households, and then failing to report this to the social services, who have the power to demand entry, must cease. To quote Dr Henry Kempe again, 'It is not lack of skill that stops health professionals ... but timidity, and inadequate back-up by local authorities and the courts. They, along with many social workers, often cannot face the fact that some parents are simply not able to be parents.'

One of the most powerful lessons to be learned from the Dutch way of dealing with abuse is that it is possible to intervene effectively and forcefully in family life without necessarily violating the independent rights of the family, except where those rights have to be abrogated in the best interests of a child.

If social services departments and health authorities do manage to forge a close working relationship in child-abuse cases, this should go a long way not only towards strengthening and expanding the capacities of both groups of workers, but also towards boosting confidence about assessing risk factors in individual cases. While they have had mainly to rely on their subjective judgement and impressions, health and social workers have often deceived themselves by lowering their own standards to fit the expectations of a particular family, and have hesitated to act until there was a crisis. In the cases of the Aziz and Page families, the lack of objective criteria allowed the children's circumstances to deteriorate very badly while the professionals continued to be optimistic. Although it would be too sweeping to recommend that medical criteria alone should be the decisive factors in determining how abuse cases should be managed, two points seem clear. First, understanding the nature and significance of these criteria would give social services departments (acting with doctors and health visitors) an accurate measure against which to judge the type of priority treatment a child should receive. Second, such understanding would enable them to intervene early and vigorously in situations where the risks to a child might otherwise be seriously underestimated.

The histories of all the cases we have reported emphasize the need for early intervention if there is to be any hope of rescuing a child from permanent trauma and of breaking the cyclical pattern of abuse. Again, a technical appreciation of the crucial stages of childhood development is very useful in lending weight to a policy which advocates swift and precise action. Often unsure professionals have allowed cases to meander along, not knowing quite when to signal a point of no return, meanwhile passing the essential milestones in a child's life. If early intervention is to be successful it requires a confident application of standards which are both objective and fair, a determination to be certain that the child's interests are paramount, and a recognition that the preservation of the biological family unit may not necessarily coincide with the child's best interests. In short, early intervention seems to involve a radical departure from most of the conventional practices of contemporary social work.

Just as it would be inappropriate to argue that management decisions should be taken solely on the basis of medical criteria, so it would be ridiculous to suggest that removing a child from its natural family should be anything other than a last resort. There have been recent fears that social services departments might respond to widespread public criticism of their methods by putting all abused children into residential care. Such so-called 'defensive' social work would cause harmfully unneccessary dislocation and distress to the vast number of families who can be kept together without their children being in serious danger. On the other hand, in extreme cases such as the Beckford or Page families, if the professionals made a rapid calculation that the parents were always going to be abusive, tragedy could be avoided by removing the children from them at an early stage. Obviously it is easy to be certain with hindsight, but it seems to be generally agreed that a child who is taken away early enough from an irremediable situation will escape abuse during the most formative years, and be able to establish alternative emotional bonds with other non-related adults.

The so-called 'permanency principle' asserts persuasively that what a child needs if he or she is to develop securely is a stable home, which may or may not be the home of his or her natural parents. This suggests that many of today's social workers may be misguided in zealously pursuing the rehabilitation of abusive families who, if they were properly assessed, could be categorized as irremediable. In the Dutch system the definition of 'irremediable' has been drawn much more narrowly than might be acceptable under some of the high-risk checklists, and such families are still kept together in residential centres like the Amsterdam Triangel. These centres, which have no exact counterparts in this country, are enormously expensive to run; one 'family centre' we visited in Newcastle cost over £800 for a family of four per week, and so far there are no long-term results on which to judge whether this level of expenditure is justified. More important, perhaps, than the economic calculation is the developmental one. If children are part of experimental rehabilitation programmes during the vital period between the ages of eighteen months and four years, there is a risk that they will suffer long-term damage if abuse continues or the rehabilitation fails.

In any case in Britain most families never experience the opportunity that a remedial family centre offers. These are the majority of high-risk cases, and it seems probable that a child from such a family who is several times fostered and then returned home on trial, only to be fostered again after a further incident of abuse, is more likely to be insecure and troubled than one who is permanently fostered or adopted at a young age. But a decision to take this irrevocable action on behalf of a child requires the kind of confident expert understanding of abuse which seems to be sadly lacking in many of the professionals working in the field today. It also requires a firm policy of giving the child's individual well-being absolute priority.

Nowhere is the need for early, decisive, specialist action greater than in the problem of sexual abuse, and yet, precisely because of the nature of this abuse, such action is even more difficult to achieve than in physical abuse and neglect. As we have seen, identifying sexual abuse depends on the disclosure by a victim that it has occurred. Even with very small children the physical signs of abuse are often not conclusive and the testimony of the child is the only sure evidence. But, because this is the most closely guarded family secret of them all, abuse may continue for many years before the victim summons enough courage to tell anyone, and by then it may be too late for his or her own sexual adjustment. As we saw in the case of Carol Broadbent, it was not until she was in her twenties, with four children of her own, that she felt able to tell the story of her grandfather molesting her as a seven-year-old; Donna Stockton was sixteen when she went to the social services to complain of her father's incest.

There are some optimistic signs that it is becoming easier for children to reveal their experiences, and that their stories are being more readily believed by the adult world. The statistics indicating an increase in the incidence of sexual abuse have shocked and alarmed the general public, but, at the same time, the fiercer spotlight has made it possible for the subject to be discussed more freely in the media and by the experts, so that victims are less reluctant to come forward. There has been a definite change in official attitudes to the traumatic difficulties experienced by children who have had to give evidence in court against accused perpetrators. In the autumn of 1986 the government promised to introduce legislation to allow child witnesses to give court evidence by live video link. But the idea that a child's original disclosure could be taped and used in court, as it is in many American states, is still treated with suspicion. The Home Secretary has said, 'In this area I must avoid action which may look good in the short term but which may on closer examination prove to be flawed.' But he has promised to keep the subject under 'close and continuing review'. The Home

Office has given its blessing to experimental investigations, where specially trained detectives and social workers act together to try and establish the truth about alleged sexual abuse, using life-like dolls to help young victims, and the experiments are being encouraged and extended.

The difficulties in changing the corroboration rules and relaxing the pompously formal atmosphere of British courts are more intractable and less susceptible to political decision. Recent experiences of many of those working in the courts are not encouraging. Dr Eileen Vizard, a psychiatrist who specializes in child sexual abuse, is spending more and more time under scrutiny in the High Court. She is far from optimistic and told us that 'there has been an intensification of attacks from some judges recently and it is very clear that there is a polarization of views about the way we interpret children's communication. But it could be that the polarization will itself crystallize the issues for debate between the specialists in child therapy and the lawyers.' There is increasing contact between members of the legal profession and the doctors and policemen who have pioneered the new methods of inquiring into child abuse, and it is to be hoped that eventually all the lawyers and judges involved in such cases will come to accept that justice is not necessarily served by discrediting a child witness in open court.

In the last year or so many education authorities have taken a lead both in informing pupils about sexual abuse and in providing situations where they may feel able to disclose what has happened to them. Independent schemes, like Kidscape, are being introduced into schools where, through role-playing and a lighthearted approach to a very serious problem, children are made to feel less guilty and more relaxed about complex family situations where they are often trapped by adults into a web of deceit and secrecy as well as sexual perversion. The extraordinary response to the telephone counselling network called Child Line which started late in 1986 was a clear indication of the need of thousands of children to tell someone about abuse. Until this national organization was formed, a few individuals had run their own confidential phone system and had been inundated with requests for help. The Child Line received 5,000 calls in the first forty-eight hours and victims from an earlier generation have talked feelingly to us about how they wish that such a system had been available to them.

The shifts which have taken place in political, administrative and legal attitudes on abuse reflect what seems to be a real change in public awareness of the problem. The instinctive revulsion and ephemeral anger which customarily greeted revelations about assaults on children is being replaced by sustained public concern and pressure to find ways of helping all children at risk. Recently, this has sometimes found expression in blanket criticism of social workers and their practices, and negative despair about the inadequacy of welfare services. But there is a growing understanding that child abuse is an extremely complex problem; this is accompanied by a genuine wish to unravel the social and psychological causes of something which is increasingly seen as a problem for which the whole community must take responsibility.

Since the Beckford report was published in the autumn of 1985, there has been a general acceptance of the fact that we are dealing with an epidemic of physical and sexual abuse and neglect. As more and more evidence emerges that the child who lives next door or the one who sits next to your own child at school may be the next victim, it is becoming impossible for anyone to pretend that reported cases are distant aberrations.

For their part those who make policy and run campaigns have become convinced of the value of drawing the general public into the struggle to prevent abuse. The DHSS document *Working Together* included the community at large in its list of those who should be involved in co-operative efforts to protect children. It speaks of the need to encourage and establish local self-help groups and voluntary counselling services, and of the importance of providing secure, confidential channels through which individuals can bring cases to the attention of the professional authorities. The guidelines make a formal recommendation that 'Social service departments should ensure that there are effective arrangements to allow members of the public to refer to them concern about individual children.' The document notes that there is evidence of public frustration at getting enmeshed in the bureaucracies of town-hall departments and telephone systems when trying to find someone who can help with a suspected case.

The NSPCC launched its latest national programme to focus

attention on neglect with special emphasis on the need for every citizen to be vigilant. The society published specific checklists of things to look out for, and urged anyone who was anxious to forget his or her reluctance to interfere in other people's business and to put the interests of the child first by calling in outside help. But the NSPCC was also keen to point out that local communities could help prevent serious cases of neglect by offering support to isolated young parents and trying to recreate some of the benefits of neighbourhood networks which in the past often sustained families suffering personal upheavals or economic hardship.

There was a horrified response when a neighbour of the Beckford family described how night after night he listened to Maurice Beckford beating his stepdaughter, heard the little girl's cries for help, and, not knowing how to intervene or whom to turn to, did nothing. But it is difficult to be totally censorious about such a dilemma – many people feel great trepidation at intruding on the sanctity of other homes and other families' lives, and have tried to escape involvement by convincing themselves that nothing serious is wrong. As knowledge about the nature and extent of child abuse spreads, and social barriers are forced lower and lower by the volume of open discussion, so, perhaps, it will become much more acceptable for citizen watchdogs actively to protect children at risk, particularly if the lines of communication with official agencies function more effectively. Nonetheless it is a narrow distinction between a responsible, caring community and a busybody, tale-telling one; it may be that the pendulum will have to swing a little too far towards the busybodies in order eventually to swing back to a position where a balance can be struck between helpful concern and unnecessary interference.

Whether or not British society will ever be prepared to lay down absolute standards for a fulfilled and happy childhood, in the way that the Dutch have done, is an open question. It is one thing to encourage a climate where individuals feel able to identify and intervene in instances of flagrant abuse, but quite another to produce a collective view of the standards of parenting and child care that society judges appropriate. Yet, as the British Association of Social Workers has pointed out in its *Policy on Child Abuse*, 'Most parents have an ability to recognize the needs of their children.... most can respond without much, or any, conscious thought or formal knowledge. "Good enough parenting" therefore can be summarized as the ability of parents to recognize (consciously or without clear understanding) and respond to the needs of their children.' The hard question for all of us, and particularly for those who have to formulate and administer general rules in this field, is how to explain those instinctive understandings to the minority who, for one reason or other, lack them. In spite of the confidence of BASW and other professionals, it seems to us that it would be advantageous, even for the majority of naturally 'good enough' parents, to receive more formal education about the basic needs and rights of children.

There are many secondary-school students, of both sexes, who would enjoy learning about the milestones of child development and child psychology, as well as the more practical topics of how to organize a house and family. This is not, of course, to suggest that a simple fifth-year course would guarantee that they would be good parents, but more information could prevent some of the 'abuse through ignorance', such as young mothers leaving children alone for long periods or punishing them severely for not reaching unrealistically high standards of behaviour or achievement. Health visitors and welfare clinics have traditionally offered a great deal of help to all parents who feel they need advice, but they, like the voluntary systems of parent-support groups which have proliferated in the last decade, tend not to reach those who are most in need. As we have seen, in so many cases the highest risks are in those families which not only fail to look for help but reject it when it is brought to them.

We come back to the vexed, central question of how we decide who those high-risk families are, and how we organize the very special help and treatment that they need. There is no question that the community and the professional agencies must develop more reliable yardsticks, so that there is greater confidence when assessing whether or not a family is irremediable. This means more research and more effective ways of ensuring that the results of the research are widely known and properly understood. Perhaps now abuse has been given political priority there will be adequate money and time for the necessary background work. We know that there will be continuing debates about the theory and practice of modern social work, and about the difficulties of meshing the best interests of the child with the exactitudes of our legal system, and we know that human nature will ensure that a gap remains between what national officials proclaim as policy and the way it is carried out at the local level. No doubt each case will continue to be so different and complex that, however well informed we become and however tightly we draw rules and definitions, we will never be able to create a general blueprint for managing a family where the children are in serious danger of abuse. But if all of us are determined to insist that in every case and at all times these children are given absolute priority by everyone involved, and that informed, authoritative decisions are taken about their lives, there is a realistic chance that their childhood will be less painful and that they will grow up to be unafflicted adults whose own children will escape the cycle of abuse. Dr Koers, the Dutch specialist, has provided the universal guideline: he simply says 'It shouldn't hurt to be a child.'